Introduction

Organizations that face harmful happenings need to react in ways that minimize or eliminate the danger…and the process by which they do this is commonly known as crisis management. Before going any further, it is important to discuss the makeup of a crisis. For the purposes of this book, an organizational crisis is defined as:

> Unanticipated events, behavior, or activities that threaten the well-being of organizations and employees

What are the basic features of a crisis? First, a crisis typically comes with little or no warning. This means that there is usually no official start time or time for preparation. Second, a crisis brings about fear in employees. This fear can be very serious…even to the point where some people fear for their lives. Third, management understands that a reaction is necessary. They are aware that sitting back and doing nothing will only make the situation worse.

Crisis management is a defense system used by management for preventing, controlling, and/or terminating situations involving a crisis. This system differs from risk management because risk management works to avoid threats while crisis management is applied after the threat has materialized. Crisis management replaces the normal day-to-day system after it is no longer effective…typically before, during, and after a dangerous situation.

Organizations typically have crisis management programs in place for emergency situations. These programs designate responses that will resolve the problems involved. The responses are important because the reputation and credibility of organizations are influenced by the way they respond to a crisis.

Now that you have a basic idea of what defines a crisis and the reasoning behind crisis management programs, let's move into a discussion on specific types of crisis situations.

Types

This refers to the different kinds of crises that occur in organizations. Specific types include:

Ethical misconduct

Ethics violations occur in organizations all over the world, and certain types of ethical misconduct can lead to crisis situations. Bribery is an example of this, and one only needs to look at the not so distant Wall Street scandals to understand the problems that ethics can create. Ethics are part of a moral compass that guides people…but sometimes it guides them in the wrong direction.

Illegal activity

Organizations that engage in illegal activity create the perfect storm for a crisis. One example is a company not paying taxes on money earned, another example is a company involved in collusion, a third example is the formation of a monopoly, and the fourth example is a company influencing the price of their stock by buying or selling it at predetermined times (sometimes based on insider information). There are many ways that illegal activity can occur, but the common denominator of all of these is the fact that they can trigger a crisis.

Technological or mechanical failure

Downed computer systems, power failures, and equipment or machinery malfunctions are all examples of technological or mechanical failures that can lead to a crisis. This type of crisis has grown in occurrence more than any other in recent years due to the dependence organizations have on technology. Some companies are virtually brought to a halt without computer-generated information. An example is a company that designs websites. If their technology is lost…then so is their business.

Financial problems

Financial issues can surface for a variety of reasons including reduced sales, theft, embezzlement, government intervention, and union strikes. If a money problem becomes too big to handle, then a crisis can result. Interestingly, some money problems result from short-term thinking that could be avoided. An example involves profitability. When immediate profit takes priority over everything else, long-term growth often gets cast aside…and companies experience financial issues that lead to a crisis.

Workplace violence

Conflict between coworkers occurs in every organization, and this is likely never going to change Functional conflict is constructive because different experiences, viewpoints, and opinions are used for problem-solving. However, dysfunctional conflict is not good….and it can turn violent. Violent conflict can escalate and turn into a crisis in a very short period of time.

Workplace violence can also come from external sources. Jilted spouses, unpaid debts, and revenge have all been known to trigger physical attacks. Emotions such as jealousy, anger, and frustration can all cause violent reactions…and that violence can occur in organizations.

Terrorism

Any act of terrorism creates an instant crisis. This includes hostage situations, physically harmed personnel, computer hacking, food contamination, water contamination, and air contamination. This type of crisis results from purposeful actions that are designed to gain some compliance, show strength, or make a point.

Natural Disasters

Natural disasters are also known as "acts of God." They consist of tornadoes, earthquakes, fires, tsunamis, hurricanes, and other uncontrollable aspects of nature. They do not always result in a crisis, but they certainly have the ability to do so. For example, a lightning strike that ignites a

The Leadership Handbook
9 Critical Topics Leaders Must Understand

Louis Bevoc, Allison Shearsett, Rachael Collinson and Nicole Edinburgh

Published by
NutriNiche System LLC

Louis Bevoc books...simple explanations of complex subjects

Crisis Management	3
CEO Mistakes	18
Consistently Inconsistent Leadership	34
Coworker Relationships	46
Delegation	63
Brainstorming	75
Hands-on Leadership	87
Psychopathic Employees	101
Drug Abuse	116

Crisis Management in Organizations
Using Real-World Examples

Introduction — 5
Types — 5
- Ethical misconduct — 5
- Illegal activity 5 — 5
- Technological or mechanical failure — 6
- Financial problems — 6
- Workplace violence — 6
- Terrorism — 6
- Natural Disasters — 6
- Miscommunication — 7

Programs — 7
- Before a crisis — 7
- After a crisis — 10

Weaknesses — 11
- Before a crisis — 11
- After a crisis — 14

Improving — 14
- Follow the program — 15
- Clearly define roles — 15
- Train the spokesperson — 15
- Train the trainer — 15
- Utilize technology — 15
- Look for change — 16

Future — 16
Summary — 16

fire in an outside dumpster does not constitute a crisis, but a crisis could arise if that fire spreads to an office building.

Miscommunication

Miscommunication can be blamed for many different problems in organizations...including crises. One employee misinterpreting what another has said might be relatively harmless, but it could also lead to a crisis. For example, an employee jokingly tells two coworkers that an angry coworker is carrying a gun. The two coworkers do not interpret the humor as intended, and they put the entire workplace into a panic mode. The police are contacted, the building is evacuated, and work ceases for the remainder of the day. Based on this, it is relatively easy to understand how miscommunication can lead to crisis situations.

Now that you understand the basic types of crises that can occur in organizations, let's move on to a discussion on the implementation of a crisis management program using real-world examples.

Programs

This section explains how crisis management programs are developed and written. It lists essential steps that must be adhered to, and it includes a food processing company example for each step. The program consists of two parts, *before the crisis* and *after the crisis*, as follows:

Before a crisis

The following steps need to be taken before a crisis occurs using a food processing company as an example.

1. Create a team

    This entails putting together a team of skilled individuals who will be in charge of all aspects of the program and handle crisis situations when they occur. The team does not need to be all management personnel, and it can include outsiders.

    Example: The food processing company sets up a team that consists of the production manager, quality manager, union steward, purchasing agent, controller, and a company attorney. This group is well-rounded and should understand the most important needs of the organization. Work phone numbers, cell phone numbers, and emails are listed so there is 24/7 access to these individuals.

2. Define the worst

    Never underestimate the potential for a crisis and plan accordingly. This means being proactive rather than reactive...and it starts with brainstorming. The crisis management team needs to meet and think about potential crises that could occur. Once these thoughts are established, possible responses can start to be formulated.

> **Example #1:** The food processing company thinks about tornados, fires, workplace violence, computer hacking, ethical violations, illegal activity, strikes, layoffs, and financial difficulties. The company is located in the Midwest, so earthquakes, tsunamis, and hurricanes are not a major concern.

Although this is rare, some crises can be planned for in advance.

> **Example #2:** The food processing company knows in advance that they are closing their bakery division. This structural move will put some employees out of work…and it could cause panic throughout the organization. The crisis management team thinks about what could happen in terms of panic. Will there be a union strike? Will key people leave the organization? Will morale and motivation be negatively impacted? All of these questions are brought into the open for discussion.

3. *Establish a spokesperson*

Someone on the crisis management team needs to be the designated contact for the outside world for any type of crisis. This person should be able to answer questions from suppliers, customers, the government, the public, and the press. It might be tempting to designate multiple people for this role, but that is typically not a good idea. People say different things and their words could contradict each other, thereby making a bad situation even worse.

> **Example:** The food processing company designates its attorney as the spokesperson. This individual is a skilled writer and speaker, and she is experienced at answering questions in difficult situations.

4. *Identify proper authorities*

This designates the authorities that will be contacted when a crisis occurs. People from these organizations are experienced in crisis situations, and they can provide assistance and advice.

> **Example:** The food processing company generates the following list of authorities that will be contacted:
>
> - Police and Fire Department
> - Water Department
> - Alarm Company
> - Rescue/Ambulance: 911
> - FBI

- Department of Homeland Security
- Government Agencies: USDA, FDA, and OSHA

5. *List potential crises*

    This defines the potential crisis that could occur. It takes the thoughts from the brainstorming (*define the worst* section) sessions and reduces those thoughts to real possibilities.

    Example: The food processing company generates the following list of potential crises:

    - Fire – natural, accidental, or arson
    - Raw material contamination – water, food ingredients (accidental or purposeful)
    - Finished product contamination – accidental or purposeful (sabotage)
    - Workforce shortages – planned (strike, walkout, etc.) or unplanned (illness, transportation, etc.)
    - Power failure – planned (sabotage) or unplanned (faulty equipment or energy loss)
    - Weather (rain, tornadoes, snow, etc.)
    - Chemical spills (cleaning, sanitizing, maintenance, etc.)
    - Governmental – food safety (USDA), workplace safety (OSHA), or financial violations (IRS)

6. *List actions taken*

    This designates what will be done when a crisis occurs. The specific crisis is identified along with the actions that will be taken.

    Example: The food processing company designates the following actions for a power failure:

    - Provide flashlights to management personnel
    - Check for trapped people in all areas (processing areas, elevators, stairways, etc.)
    - Evacuate the building (if necessary)
    - Call emergency contacts as determined necessary (refrigeration contractor, electrician, electric and gas companies, etc.)
    - Conduct an onsite inspection to determine where outage exists, and try to find out when power will be restored
    - Shut down all equipment that could be damaged
    - Cover exposed product and keep all cooler/refrigerator/freezer doors closed
    - Monitor products for food safety concerns

- Document all injuries/incidents/expenses incurred

7. *Train affected personnel*

    Normally, this means training the members of the crisis management team. However, all employees might require some type of training process to educate them on the potential for a crisis, the actions taken during a crisis, and the effects of a crisis.

    Example: The food processing company holds an annual training session with the crisis management team. An outside consultant facilitates the meeting and gears the content toward the specific needs of the company. A test is given at the end of the meeting and all team members must answer 100 percent of the questions properly, or they are retrained and retested until they fully comprehend the subject matter.

After a crisis

The following steps need to be taken after a crisis occurs using the food processing company as an example.

8. *Assess*

    This refers to assessing the damage that was done during the crisis. Questions that need to be answered include: Was equipment damaged? Was product damaged? Was property damaged? Were people injured?

    Example (for a fire): A fire occurred at the food processing company's pasta plant. All of the equipment in the packaging area was destroyed, but the rest of the plant had little damage. Fortunately, nobody was injured.

9. *Gather feedback*

    After a crisis is over and done, management needs to gather information. This information can be used to understand better why the crisis occurred, and it can potentially be used to prevent a reoccurrence.

    Example (for a fire): The food processor asks questions about the fire to police and fire investigators. Fire investigators determine that the problem came from faulty wiring. This means terrorism and sabotage can be ruled out, and it also means electricians need to take appropriate action to prevent this from happening again.

Crisis management programs are designed to combat any type of crisis, but they are not foolproof. Something can go wrong or the plan simply might not work. Whatever the case, these programs often have weaknesses....and those weaknesses are discussed in the next section.

Weaknesses

Below are weak points of crisis management programs that often render those plans ineffective.

Before a crisis:

The following are weak points of crisis management programs before a crisis occurs using the food processing company as an example:

- *Importance*

    This might be the most common weakness. It occurs when programs are not considered important to top management. If this is the case, then these programs will not be taken seriously by employees, and they could fail when needed.

    Example: Assume the CEO of the food processing company does not get involved with the crisis management program. He tells his vice presidents to implement the program, and they pass the responsibility on to their managers. There is no commitment from upper management, so the crisis management team does not place a high level of importance on the program. It is thought of as just another directive from upper management...so the team merely goes through the motions of implementation.

- *Brainstorming*

    This refers to a lack of effort given to thinking about crises that could occur. All potential crises need to be taken into consideration, and this requires some serious brainstorming. Crisis management teams that take this responsibility lightly could be headed for big problems later on.

    Example: The production manager, quality manager, union steward, purchasing agent, controller, and company attorney make up the food processing company's crisis management team. Assume that the lawyer and controller are "too busy" to make it to the brainstorming meetings. Their absence means potential financial and legal crises are not being considered...and this means that the other member's brainstorming is incomplete.

- *Application*

This refers to a crisis management program being too generic. It happens when organizations fail to tailor a program to their individual needs.

> **Example:** Assume the crisis management team at the food processing company obtains a crisis management program from the internet that uses an automotive manufacturer as an example. This is a good start since manufacturing is a common dominator. However, the team fails to modify the program to meet the needs of the company. For example, the automotive program has a heavy focus on machinery and equipment crises that can occur on the manufacturing floor. This applies to the food processing company, but they need most of their focus to be on food safety…something the automotive manufacturer does not take into consideration.

- *Delegation*

This weakness occurs when the responsibilities of crisis management teams are not designated. Team members are unsure of what they need to do because nothing has been delegated.

> **Example**: Assume the food processing company selects the team members, but does not assign responsibilities to any of them. This creates confusion and fighting over who will do what…and eventually, everyone stops communicating. In short, the program has failed before it has a chance to get off the ground.

- *Clarity*

This weakness occurs when the responsibilities of crisis management teams are not clearly designated. This differs from the delegation weakness because team members are told what they need to do, but they are not given any details. In other words, the assigned responsibilities lack clarity.

> **Example:** Assume all members of the crisis management team at the food processing company have been assigned responsibilities. The purchasing agent has been charged with making sure money is available for any type of crisis. However, she is left confused because no other direction is given. How much money should be available? Where does this money need to be held? Who should have access to this money? When should the money be released? Nothing has been clarified, so there is ample room for misunderstanding and confusion.

- *Communication*

This weakness should not come as a surprise to anyone who has worked for a business. Communication is critical for the efficient operation of virtually every aspect of business, and crisis management is no exception. Without good communication, crisis management programs fail to be successful...before or after the crisis.

> **Example #1:** Assume the crisis management team at the food processing company is established by upper management. Individual responsibilities have been assigned, and the implementation of the program seems to be going fairly well. However, team members are not communicating with each other. Each member has some good ideas, but they do not discuss those ideas as a group. There is no defining of potential crises or documentation of actions that will be taken because the team does not meet regularly for discussion. Eventually, the crisis management program is abandoned due to what appears to be a lack of interest...but the problem actually stems from a lack of communication.

A crisis management program can also fail due to a lack of commutation with the outside world. During a crisis, outsiders such as police and firefighters need to be contacted to help resolve the problem. If there is a lack of communication with outsiders, then the program will not be successful

> **Example #2:** Assume the food processing company finds out that a broken water main has caused a "boil alert" for their sausage manufacturing plant. They go into crisis mode and do not make any sausage products with the contaminated water. After the water is deemed safe by local authorities, they go back to normal production. However, they did not contact the United States Department of Agriculture (USDA) about the problem. When an inspector arrives, she condemns all sausage made during the crisis because USDA was not notified. The sausage cannot be released for sale to the public due to a lack of communication with an outsider.

- *Training*

"Practice makes perfect" is a saying that has been around for many years. It can be applied to crisis management programs because, without practice, these programs will most likely fail when they are needed most. This practice comes in the form of training that prepares employees for crisis situations that could take place. Unfortunately, many organizations with solid crisis management programs fail to train...and they are not prepared for emergency situations.

> **Example:** Assume the food processing company has a good crisis management program in place. They take a generic program and tailor it to their specific needs, but they fail to implement any type of training. They do not conduct practice runs, so people are unsure of what they need to do when a real crisis occurs. This lack of training jeopardizes the value of the crisis management program, and it reflects poorly on the leadership of the organization.

After a crisis

The following are weak points of crisis management programs after a crisis occurs using the food processing company as an example:

- *Evaluation*

    Some organizations fail to assess the damage done after a crisis has occurred. Evaluation is critical because it puts a cost on the crisis…and high costs are great motivation for taking the necessary steps to prevent the same crisis from happening again.

    Example: Assume the food processing company has a power failure. They go into crisis mode and resolve the problem, but they do not assess the damage done. They know that they did not lose any product during the crisis, so they do not document any losses other than production time and labor. Unfortunately, they fail to note that the power outage caused a "brown out," and the irregular voltage destroyed electrical components in some of the manufacturing machinery. This damage could have been avoided if the machinery was turned off, but nobody has been made aware of this fact. This means a power outage could again cause a "brown out" that does the same type of damage to the electrical components of some manufacturing machinery.

- *Information*

    Information is necessary to prevent problems from reoccurring. However, some organizations fail to gather that information…and they end up in the same crisis situation.

    Example: Assume the food processing company has a power failure that puts them in a crisis situation. They determine the power failure was due to a malfunctioning transformer, so they get that transformer repaired. However, they fail to get feedback from everyone involved in the incident. They do not discuss the problem with the power company, and the power company has valuable information that could have been shared. They know that the transformer malfunction was due to water damage from rain, and a simple cover would prevent it from happening again. Without this information, the food processing company will likely encounter the same crisis in the future.

Now you are aware of some of the weaknesses of crisis management programs. These programs are now routinely implemented in organizations, so they need to be improved…and the next section focuses on their improvement.

Improving

Most organizations will face a crisis at some time, and this means they need to be prepared by having some type of plan in place. That plan is known as a crisis management program…something many companies have already implemented. However, one problem with these programs is the fact that they are usually not as good as they could be. In other words, they could use some improvement…and some important suggestions for that improvement include:

Follow the program

This is the most basic suggestion. Many crisis management programs work well when they are accurately followed, but this is often not the case. When a crisis occurs, employees tend to react from instinct and do what they feel is best at the moment. These individuals are in a panic mode, and they make decisions that reflect their panic. Unfortunately, wrong decisions are usually made…and everyone suffers. In short, crisis management programs are developed based on thought and sound principles, and they must be followed to be effective.

Clearly define roles

This refers to the crisis management team. If team members are not sure what they need to do, then the program will not be effective. Individual team members need their roles defined so they can take on the responsibilities that go with those roles. When there is clarity, confusion is eliminated and members work together toward a common goal. As noted earlier, lack of communication is a weakness for crisis management programs…and clarity helps to eliminate that weakness.

Train the spokesperson

Spokespeople might be gifted writers or speakers, but they can still write or say the wrong things. They need to be prepared to cover the necessary bases and prevent bad information from leaving organizations. This preparation needs to encompass all the necessary "dos" and "don'ts" of communication during a crisis…including the use of social media. The crisis itself is a major problem…and communication mishaps add to that problem. In short, a little time spent training the spokesperson can prevent many problems during a crisis.

Train the trainer

Typically, someone in the organization takes a lead role in training personnel. This trainer makes sure members of the crisis management team understand their roles and he or she oversees all practice runs. Unfortunately, many times the person in the lead role does not have the necessary experience to take charge. If this is the case, organizations need to invest in outside firms that specialize in "training the trainer" for crisis management.

Utilize technology

Technology is constantly progressing, and it needs to be taken advantage of in crisis management programs. For example, cell phones can be equipped with apps that alert team members when crises occur. This is much better than hoping that they are by their computers to receive an email or trying to call or text multiple parties. Another example involves camera capabilities. Activities in organizations can be viewed from any computerized device with internet access, and findings can be used to streamline crisis resolution. In short, technology works to identify and resolve crises more efficiently and effectively, and its value cannot be ignored or underestimated.

Look for change

Crisis management programs need to be followed…but this does not mean that they need to remain the same. Organizations always undergo change, and they need to adjust their crisis management programs accordingly. This process should be proactive where organizations are constantly asking what works and what does not. Change takes employees out of their comfort zones, but it is necessary to improve crisis management programs. Unfortunately, many people will not accept change unless they are required to do so; and this hinders their personal and professional growth. As one astute business leader jokingly stated, "the only change my employees accept is an increase in their paycheck….and that is only if it does not put them in a higher tax bracket."

Now you understand some ways that crisis management programs can be improved. Let's move on to the next section that highlights the importance of crisis management by discussing its role in the future.

Future

Nobody has a crystal ball to predict the future, but it is fairly safe to assume that crisis management programs will become more common in all types of organizations. Some of these programs will be implemented voluntarily, but others will be mandated by government regulations. Crises will arise, and they will need to be dealt with as efficiently as possible.

For food processing companies, crisis management programs likely will be made mandatory by the Food and Drug Administration (FDA), USDA, and state and local health departments. This is due to food safety concerns for the general public. Government authorities do not want to release adulterated or contaminated products into the food supply chain for fear of people getting sick…and possibly even dying.

Summary

More and more leaders are realizing that crisis management is important to the growth and survival of their organizations. This importance will grow in the future, and it means the proper implementation and maintenance of crisis management programs will also become more significant.

This book focuses on crisis management in organizations. It explores different types of crises, shows how to set up crisis management programs, examines the weaknesses of these programs, suggests methods for improving these programs, and discusses the future of crisis management in general. Real-world examples are used for illustration and exemplification purposes, and the text is written for easy understanding at any reading level.

Congratulations! You now understand more about crisis management...an increasingly important aspect of planning for organizations all over the world.

CEO Mistakes in Organizations

Introduction

- 1-49 employees ... 19
- 50-199 employees ... 19
- 200-999 employees ... 19
- 1000 or more employees ... 21

Importance

- CEOs make decisions ... 21
- CEOs take risks ... 21
- CEOs provide leadership ... 22
- CEOs build teams ... 22
- CEOs provide vision ... 22
- CEOs establish culture ... 23

Indicators of success

- Employees ... 23
- Customers ... 24
- Board of directors ... 24
- General public ... 24

Mistakes

- Unwillingness to admit problems ... 25
- Unwillingness to accept advice ... 25
- Unwillingness to utilize feedback ... 25
- Unwillingness to accept responsibility ... 26
- Unwillingness to sacrifice profitability ... 26
- Unwillingness to display emotions ... 27
- Unwillingness to encourage innovation ... 28
- Unwillingness to build trust ... 28
- Unwillingness to establish a positive culture ... 28
- Unwillingness to motivate ... 29
- Unwillingness to set realistic expectations ... 29
- Unwillingness to gain a full understanding ... 30
- Narcissism ... 30
- Favoritism ... 30
- Nepotism ... 31
- Micromanagement ... 31

Summary ... 32

Introduction

It is only fair to start this book by setting parameters regarding the size of the organizations. Organizations vary widely in the number of people they employ, and the roles of CEOs are often dictated by those numbers. For example, a CEO with 10 employees has different responsibilities than a CEO with 1000 employees.

The following looks at the number of employees in workplaces and the roles CEOs play in those organizations:

1-49 employees

In addition to running the organization, CEOs with less than 50 employees often have to work in it. This means they might have to jump onto a manufacturing line, make deliveries, process customer orders, provide IT support, and/or hire and terminate personnel. Their role is that of a manager and worker, and they focus on doing whatever is necessary to keep the business operating.

These CEOs often do not have the time or resources to focus on long-term growth or expansion. Their hands are often full due to the wearing of multiple hats, and it is not uncommon for them to put in workweeks of 70 or more hours. They live their businesses and have grass roots understanding of what it takes to run them. These CEOs personify their organizations, and this is reflected in every business decision.

50-199 employees

At this level, CEOs begin to focus more on running the business rather than working it. They generate ideas for growth and set goals. While these leaders are no longer tied to individual jobs, they are still on the ground floor of their operations. Some of their authority is delegated to managers, but they are still involved in many of the day-to-day decisions that need to be made.

This size is advantageous because CEOs fully understand their organizations because they are entrenched in everyday operations. However, it also has limitations because CEOs are not able to focus the majority of their time on growth and direction.

200-999 employees

When organizations reach this size, CEOs truly begin to delegate. They are no longer involved in day-to-day decision-making, instead focusing on the growth of the organization. They spend their time meeting with managers who implement policies, programs, and procedures for the lower-level employees.

This size is advantageous because CEOs can focus on the large picture of their organizations, but it also has limitations because they lose touch with what is happening operationally. Regardless of the good or bad involved, this is the point where CEOs start to fit the stereotype associated with them by many people.

1000 or more employees

At this point, CEOs delegate virtually all of their responsibilities because they have the resources available to do so. Their focus is strategic and their role is that of a visionary for the direction of the company.

This size is advantageous because smart CEO decisions can lead to growth levels that are virtually impossible for smaller organizations. However, poor CEO decision making can lead to the destruction of organizations and the loss of jobs for thousands of employees

This book focuses on mistakes made by CEOs in organizations with 1000 or more employees. This does not mean that these CEOs make more or less mistakes than their counterparts in smaller organizations...it is simply a reference point for comparing apples to apples.

Now that you understand the parameters of this book, we can move forward to the major content....mistakes of CEOs. However, before we do this, we need to discuss (1) the importance of CEOs and (2) the indicators of their success. Let's start with the importance of CEOs in organizations.

Importance

Are CEOs important to organizations? The answer is almost always "yes," but that importance is for different reasons. These reasons are as follows:

CEOs make decisions

Most CEOs reach their position because they are skilled at making decisions. When they attain the top job in an organization, that decision skill becomes even more important. Their decisions impact the direction of the company and many people's livelihoods. In this sense, their decision-making is more important than every other employee.

Involvement often determines decision-making. CEOs who are actively involved understand the needs of their organizations and react appropriately. They make decisions based on the information they have available, and those decisions bring about the change necessary for growth and prosperity.

In short, decision-making by CEOs affects the survival and well-being of their organizations...and this shows their importance to those organizations.

CEOs take risks

Decisions that drive organizations often come with risk...and risk is something that most CEOs are not afraid to take. They will go out on a limb if they believe it will be beneficial. This is good because risk-taking is often essential for organizational success. In fact, most large companies would not be that size if leaders had not gambled at some point.

The downside of risk is that it can have devastating consequences if the CEO is wrong. The resulting problems can affect every employee and result in a negative perception of the workplace. In other words, risk jeopardizes the well-being of organizations.

Regardless of the end result, risk is necessary for most organizations, and CEOs are not afraid to gamble if they believe they are making the right decision. This makes them very important to the operations they direct.

CEOs provide leadership

Managers run the day-to-day operations of organizations. They assign specific people to jobs to achieve designated goals. They implement and uphold policies and procedures to make sure order is maintained. They play the role of watchdogs and overseers as organizations progress and move forward.

Managers, however, are not true leaders. True leaders develop the goals that managers seek to attain, and they establish the policies and procedures that managers implement and uphold. Managers need direction…and that direction comes from CEOs. This is why the term CEO is synonymous with leadership…and it is also why CEOS are important to organizations.

CEOs build teams

Teams are major building blocks of organizations. They have replaced individuals in an attempt to satisfy complex customer demands and resolve internal issues. Employees are selected for teams based on their position, skill, knowledge, and capacity to lead others. The assembled group is well equipped to find solutions to problems based on their experience, understanding, and capability.

CEOs are responsible for selecting executive teams. They choose members based on their skill levels and their ability to exchange thoughts and entertain other perspectives. CEOs understand the fact that the synergy of executive teams improves decision-making and increases the likelihood that goals and objectives will be achieved. Executive teams are very important organizations….and so are the CEOs that establish them.

CEOs provide vision

Everyone is not capable of visualizing what needs to be done to achieve success, especially when it involves large organizations that employ thousands of people. Most employees look to others to determine future direction because they are unsure about what could happen or they fear potential backlash from making the wrong move. This is acceptable for most jobs…but someone has to take the "bull by the horns" and make decisions about the future.

CEOs look into the future, see potential, and turn that potential into reality. They are skilled at communicating their vision to others to establish the direction of workplaces. They help employees realize the value of change in terms of growth and prosperity. CEOs are visionaries, and this makes them important to the organizations that employ them.

CEOs establish culture

All organizations have unique experiences, philosophies, behaviors, norms, and values. They also have specific methods and patterns for interacting with suppliers, customers, employees, and the community. When combined, these attributes define an organization and make up its culture.

Culture starts at the top of an organization and works its way down into the rank and file. Employees can help establish behaviors and norms, but they do not have the same power as those in the upper levels of the established hierarchy. High-ranking members are the only people who have the authority, influence, and control needed to create the overall culture of the organization.

CEOs are the highest-ranking members in organizations. They define the culture and purpose of workplaces. This influences productivity, performance, service, and quality….and it highlights the importance of CEOs to their organizations.

As you can see, CEOs are important to organizations, but this leads to another question. How do we know if they have been successful? That question is answered in the next section.

Indicators of success

What makes CEOs of large organizations successful? The answer can be found in feedback given by employees, customers, the board of directors, and the general public. The following is a more detailed look at each of these indicators:

Employees

This would likely be the most accurate indicator…if the employees were honest with their input. Honest employees would address CEO's strengths and weaknesses, thereby exposing them to the people who can make changes at the top of the organization (board members and stockholders). However, most employees are not honest about their evaluation of CEOs. They disclose only the positive aspects of CEOs for the following two reasons:

They do not want change

Some employees do not want change because they do not want to jeopardize the status of their current positions. Top managers might risk losing good positions that come with sizeable salaries and bonuses by negatively evaluating their CEOs. This is not due to retaliation…in fact, it is the opposite. These employees do not want their CEOs to lose power or be removed because their jobs will be negatively impacted.

They fear retaliation

This is likely the most common reason that employees do not give negative feedback about CEOs. They fear their derogatory comments could be held against them by their CEO or other top managers. If this is the case, then they risk demotion or job loss...so it is simply not worth it.

Customers

Customers are often the most critical indicators of CEO success. They determine the survival and growth of organizations by purchasing their products and/or services. They base their opinions of CEOs on quality and service. If quality and service are good, then it is likely that they will have a positive view of the organization and the CEO who runs it. If quality and service are poor, then the CEO stands little chance of being perceived as successful.

The problem with customers determining the success of CEOs is the fact that their viewpoints are largely one-dimensional. As might be expected, they only take certain factors into account while ignoring many others. For example, they are not concerned about how CEOs treat their employees, how they deal with board members, or how they react to internal conflict. They are only concerned with the quality and service of their purchases...and this does not present a complete picture of the CEO's success.

Board of directors

These people do a good job evaluating the CEO's financial performance because they get to the bottom line. In short, they look at profits and stock prices. These factors tell a lot about the financial well-being of the organization, and they are the direct responsibility of CEOs.

Unfortunately, there are problems when boards of directors assess the success of CEOs. These individuals are too far removed from the day-to-day operations to make educated analyses of the situation. They often base their opinions solely on financial aspects...but those aspects do not paint a complete picture of CEO performances.

General public

Public perception is very powerful, and it can make or break companies and the CEOs that are in charge of them. When perception is good, CEOs are thought of as being successful...but that level of success declines sharply when perception is bad. Regardless of the positive or negative perception, the general public is a strong indicator of the CEO's success.

Unfortunately, the general public is by far the most uninformed indicator of CEO success because their opinions are often based on what they read online or in newspapers and magazines. Sometimes this information is not all fact, and other times it only involves financial aspects or ethical concerns of organizations. Either way, the information is incomplete and it does not justify a conclusion about the success of CEOs.

Now you have an understanding of the ways CEOs' success is measured. Keeping this information in mind, it is time to move into the major focus of this book....mistakes of CEOs.

Mistakes

Every employee makes mistakes, but the majority of those mistakes are rarely as visible as the ones made by CEOs. This is because CEOs are at the top, and they are expected to do things right. They are compensated handsomely for their efforts, and that compensation comes with a big responsibility. Part of that responsibility entails doing things correctly for employees and the organization…but this is not always possible.

The following are mistakes that CEOs have been known to make along with the resulting consequences:

Unwillingness to admit problems

By nature, CEOs are very optimistic. This is a good thing because most people do not want pessimists in charge of their organizations. They also want people in the top positions to be upbeat because, after all, the feelings of CEOs eventually tickle down and affect the rank and file employees.

There are, however, times when CEOs are overly optimistic because they are unwilling to admit there are problems. In these situations, they are looking at what they hope will transpire instead of the reality of the situation. Employees are kept in the dark on important matters, and this can create problems instead of preventing them. Additionally, it is not fair to workers who are told their company is doing great when it is really about to close its doors.

False optimism also prevents employees from moving into a crisis mentality, and sometimes this mindset is necessary to get out of bad situations. Financial instability, for example, requires employees to look hard at their departments to find ways where cost-saving measures can be applied. If they are not told there are money problems, then they will not change anything…and something needs to change to prevent further economic downfall.

Unwillingness to accept advice

CEOs in large companies are usually quite knowledgeable. They have worked a variety of jobs and understand what it takes for their organizations to function effectively and efficiently. They also understand what it takes to get the job done and have been successful the vast majority of their careers. They know a lot, but they do not know everything.

A major mistake CEOs make is thinking that they know everything. Regardless of their knowledge, they should always be open to advice from others. Many employees have jobs that deal with specifics of the organization that are not fully understood by CEOs. Those employees are willing to share their experience…as long as someone will listen to them.

Unwillingness to utilize feedback

Feedback from employees, customers, suppliers, and others is a very valuable tool for making changes and improving organizations. However, that feedback is only useful if it is realized and put into action. CEOs who receive feedback and never use it are making a huge mistake...and that mistake will be very apparent over time.

Unwillingness to delegate

CEOs who try to do everything by themselves will not be successful. They need to continually delegate to accomplish organizational goals and objectives...and some make the mistake of not doing this.

Delegation is a major key to the success of organizations. When CEOs delegate, they relieve some of their workload; thereby allowing them to focus on other tasks. Additionally, those on the receiving end of the delegation become more interested in work because their jobs are more challenging.

When work is delegated by CEOs, productivity increases. This is because work is broken down into manageable portions that are given to different employees. Psychologically, this is easier than handling an entire project because people are not faced with an overwhelming amount of work that needs to be finished. They see a small of work, and this inspires them to get it done.

Delegation also gives employees decision-making power. This power results in employees taking responsibility for the jobs they are performing, and that responsibility commits them to the goals and objectives of the organization.

One of the best things about CEO delegation is that it allows employees to learn. They are assigned a task, and they are responsible for following that task through to completion. This takes time and effort, but it also provides a real-world learning experience that cannot be obtained by reading a book or sitting in a classroom.

Unwillingness to accept responsibility

As noted earlier, every employee makes mistakes. However, often times the actual mistake takes a backseat to the way it is handled. Do the people who committed the mistake own up to it or deny it was their fault? When employees do not take responsibility for their wrong actions, their coworkers lose respect for them.

In the case of CEOs, their unwillingness to accept responsibility for their mistakes can negatively impact all employees. For example, A CEO who promises bonuses that do not transpire due to her profitability calculation error disappoints many employees. If she tries to blame the accounting department for her mistake, she adds anger and outrage to an already upset workforce. Obviously, not all situations are as dramatic as this example, but the point is clear that CEOs add to their mistakes if they do not own up to them.

Unwillingness to sacrifice profitability

It is true that money talks. In fact, it talks very loudly...and CEOs find it difficult to not listen because their organizations are driven by profitability. Investors, stockholders, analysts, unions, customers, suppliers, unions, and employees all watch the financial standing of the organizations they are associated with, and this puts a lot of pressure on the individuals in charge.

Many CEOs refuse to look past profitability. They want the bottom line to be impressive so they can get people off their backs and reward themselves handsomely. Unfortunately, their refusal to see anything other than profits is a mistake because sometimes short-term sacrifice is necessary to build for the future. CEOs who fail to see the big picture are risking the longevity of their organizations. They need to keep in mind that the people who are happy with their performance now might be the same ones calling for their resignation in the near future.

Unwillingness to display emotions

Emotional intelligence is the ability to recognize emotions, classify them, and use them to influence people's behavior. People with high emotional intelligence are sympathetic, empathetic, and thoughtful toward others. They also know how to temper their own feelings and react rationally to situations that might involve irrational behavior.

CEOs who refuse to show compassion, sympathy, and empathy are making a big mistake for the following reasons:

- High emotional intelligence makes CEOs better leaders due to the understanding they have for employees. They create harmony at work and make sound judgments when conflicts arise. They put people at ease, gain trust, and develop positive attitudes that help drive the organization toward its missions and goals. When employees feel valued, appreciated, respected, and listened to, they are motivated to help themselves and their organizations become successful.

- Positive employee emotions benefit productivity in the workplace. They enhance people's capacity to influence others in ways that promote effectiveness and efficiency. Positive emotions tend to be contagious, and this is good for organizations. CEOs who instill positive emotions in employees are considerably more successful than those who do not.

- Innovation and creativity are critical for CEOs. Emotions influence their ability to think and come up with new ideas and concepts. Negative emotions drain the energy necessary for solid decision-making and result in CEOs becoming less original. Positive emotions act as a catalyst for confident decision-making, and they stimulate creative CEO thinking.

- Longevity and retention of employees are both important to CEOs. Employees who are satisfied with their jobs speak highly of their employer, are satisfied with their work, and remain at their jobs. Negative emotions produce job dissatisfaction and turn the organization into a revolving door for employees. Essentially, happy employees stay at their jobs while unhappy employees look for other opportunities.

In short, positive emotional displays help CEOs keep their composure, make good decisions, and connect with their employees. They listen to their worker's needs and respond in ways that make them feel better about themselves and their positions in organizations. The end result is a win-win for employees and organizations because people are happy and goals are accomplished.

Unwillingness to encourage innovation

Some people think that innovation is only important for technology-based companies. While it is critical for these types of businesses, it also has significance in virtually every other industry. No organization wants to become obsolete, and to avoid this they need to be innovative. Innovation drives people to work harder, and that is why innovative organizations have more productive employees.

Employees that work for innovative organizations are also more likely to be creative because they know their ideas will be followed through. This gets creative juices flowing and opens doors to new ways of thinking.

In short, organizations need innovation to grow and prosper. CEOs who do not make an effort to encourage innovation are preventing their organizations from continually improving.

Unwillingness to build trust

As many people are aware, trust-building is a challenging endeavor. It takes time and effort to build the relationships necessary to establish trust, and that trust can be broken with a single action.

Communication is the biggest factor involved in building trust, and it starts with CEOs. Employees lose trust when CEOs do not communicate with them. They want truthful information about the organization so they know what is happening within it. Without CEO communication, employees are lost without a guide.

Unwillingness to establish a positive culture

Every organization has unique experiences, philosophies, behaviors, norms, and values. They also have specific methods and patterns for interacting with suppliers, customers, employees, and the community. When combined, these attributes define an organization and make up its culture.

Culture starts at the top of an organization and works its way down to lower-level employees. Employees help establish behaviors and norms, but they do not have the same power as those in the upper levels of the established hierarchy. Top ranking members are the only people who have the authority, influence, and control needed to create the overall culture of the organization. CEOs who are unwilling to work toward creating a positive culture are making a mistake for the following reasons:

- Effective decision-making is critical for the survival of an organization, and that decision-making is almost always influenced by culture. Employees think about their organization's norms and values before deciding the direction to proceed. If they go against those norms and values, they risk bringing about change that might be resisted by coworkers or rejected by higher management.

- Employees' commitment to the goals and objectives of organizations is linked to their perception of the culture. Those who perceive the culture as negative are less committed than those who perceive it as positive. Committed employees identify with organizations, and this leads to better workplace culture.

- In organizations, values are very important. They influence people's decisions and behavior, and they establish norms for the entire workplace. Values are the foundation of organizational culture, and they establish patterns that employees follow while performing everyday tasks.

    Values originate from leadership. Their importance cannot be underestimated because they have a direct impact on significant aspects of organizational behavior including performance and ethics. For organizations to be successful, leadership needs to align employee values and organizational values. Employees need to identify with the organization if they are expected to work toward achieving its goals and objectives.

In short, positive culture is critical to the success of organizations, and it starts with CEOs. Those who are unwilling to build positive cultures are jeopardizing the well-being of the workplaces they reside over.

Unwillingness to motivate

Everyone needs motivation at some point in their career, and CEOs are often the best people to provide that motivation. They are at the top of the company, and their comments are taken very seriously by all employees. A pat on the back goes a long way…especially when it comes from a CEO.

CEOs who choose not to focus on motivating their employees are doing their organizations serious injustice. Unmotivated workers do not perform to the best of their abilities, thereby hindering the accomplishment of organizational goals and objectives. The chain reaction caused by this type of CEO behavior has a detrimental effect on the entire workplace…just ask anyone who has worked for an organization that failed to provide motivation.

There is, however, a bright side to this type of CEO mistake. The bright side is the fact that the negative effects can be reversed. All it takes is a little time and effort on the part of the CEO.

Unwillingness to set realistic expectations

The negative fallout from this CEO mistake is two-fold. First, unrealistic expectations mean employees can expect to fail. For example, a CEO who sets a goal for every employee in a steel manufacturing plant to lift 200 lb blocks of steel within three months is living in a dream world. There is no way that 100 lb woman can be expected to lift 200 lbs…not now, and not in the future.

Second, unrealistic expectations lead to other failures because people lose the desire to do their jobs to the best of their ability. For example, A CEO who sets a goal for every salesperson to double their sales volume after a 20 percent price increase causes his salespeople to lose trust in his ability to lead. This causes the salespeople to expect his future goals to be just as outrageous, and they eventually look elsewhere for employment.

In short, CEOs who set unrealistic expectations are making a mistake that has rippling effects. Goals will not be accomplished and other problems will result.

Unwillingness to gain a full understanding

Another mistake CEOs make is commonly known as "jumping the gun." They don't allow enough time to gather important information before making decisions…and those decisions can impact entire organizations.

One problem with this type of mistake is that sometimes it is difficult to reverse. For example, a food processing CEO signs a contract to purchase three expensive packaging machines for the packaging department. After the fact, he finds out that these machines cannot run two different products at the same time, and this was one of the major reasons that they were purchased. He signed the contract prior to having a final discussion with his plant manager, who knew the limitations of the machines. At this point, the contract is completed…and it will be difficult to negate it.

Narcissism

Narcissism is a fairly common trait in CEOs of large companies. They know they are "the best of the best" and, because of this, they were selected over many other talented people for the top position in the organization.

Unfortunately, the feeling of superiority dramatically inflates the egos of some CEOs, and this shows in many different ways. They tend to disrespect other employees by disregarding their thoughts and ideas and talking to them condescendingly. They see others as inferior and view themselves as the only people capable of leading the organizations that employ them. In many instances, CEOs are the best choice to lead their organizations, but they need to let others come to this conclusion by witnessing positive actions rather than hearing negative comments.

Narcissistic CEOs are very destructive in workplaces. Employees tend to avoid them, and this causes a lack of communication. When communication is lacking, tasks fail to get accomplished and organizational goals and objectives are not achieved. This is best summed up by making it clear that narcissistic behavior is a huge mistake of CEOs…and it should be avoided at all times.

Favoritism

CEOs who favor certain employees are making a mistake because:

- Favoritism creates jealousy and resentment and results in people not working together to complete tasks. It also demotivates people, and demotivated employees lose interest in their jobs. They are frustrated, tend to spend a good deal of their time complaining, and absenteeism is sometimes an issue. This type of behavior results in a lack of productivity, and the bottom line is negatively impacted.

- Favoritism brings about a feeling of unfairness. Employees are unhappy when they feel that they are being treated unfairly. If they see coworkers treated in special ways, they feel resentment and hostility. Favoritism opens the floodgates to an unhappy workforce, and any employee who has experienced it knows the feeling firsthand.

- Favoritism results in a lack of recognition, and lack of recognition is one sure way to lower employee morale. When employees' morale is lowered, their drive to achieve organizational goals is decreased, and their job satisfaction diminishes.

- Favoritism reduces loyalty. Loyalty is a feeling of commitment or support towards someone or something. In workplaces, this means feeling committed to the goals of the organization. When people experience favoritism, they often become less loyal to their organizations. Unfortunately, this might be the worst negative effect of favoritism because people who lose loyalty often look for other employment.

Nepotism

Similar to favoritism, nepotism can also lead to problems because the relatives who benefit have typically not earned the privilege. They are rewarded due to "who they are" rather than "what they have achieved." This means more qualified workers are passed over simply because they are not related to those in charge.

CEOs who promote nepotism are making a mistake, and good employees leave organizations because of it.

Micromanagement

Micromanagement is never good. It is particularly bad for CEOs...yet some of them still make the mistake of doing it. Reasons micromanagement is bad at the CEO level include:

- CEOs do not have the time to micromanage. They should be working on important aspects of their organizations, and micromanagement of employees is not an important aspect.

- CEOs create a lot more work for themselves when they oversee every detail of their employees' jobs. At some point, this workload will become unbearable and stress will result. That stress is not good for the CEOs or their organizations.

- Employees become less productive when they are micromanaged by CEOs. This is because they spend less time doing actual work than they do waiting for CEOs to approve every task they complete.

- CEOs who are heavy micromanagers can literally bring productivity to a halt as employees wait in line for approval.

- Micromanaged employees lose motivation due to the restrictions placed on them by CEOs. When employees are not motivated, they do not perform to the best of their abilities. Lack of performance affects the bottom line because organizational efficiency suffers.

- Empowered employees are more involved employees because they take ownership of their jobs. Micromanaged employees are not able to take ownership of their jobs. They are not empowered because CEOs dictate their actions and make decisions for them.

- Employees who are not able to make decisions in their jobs often become frustrated. If that frustration continues for prolonged periods, those employees begin to look for other positions where they can make decisions. In this sense, CEO micromanagement prevents employees from finding job satisfaction, and that lack of job satisfaction leads to turnover.

- Employees who are micromanaged by CEOs are prevented from learning new skills due to the controls imposed on them. Consequently, they never reach their potential for growth in organizations.

- Micromanaging CEOs restrict their employees' freedom and prevent them from being creative. When this happens, organizations lose the potential for novel thinking that could make processes and procedures better, less expensive, or more efficient.

- Similar to creativity, innovation also requires freedom. When employees are micromanaged by CEOs, that freedom comes with a very short leash that prevents them from using original thinking to come up with new ideas. Once again, organizations lose opportunities to get better.

- Workplace collaboration is the sharing of thoughts and ideas between coworkers. Micromanaged employees are led every step of the way, and their thinking is not shared with others unless they are told to do so by CEOs. This puts collaboration at a standstill, and it does little to help organizations grow and prosper.

CEOs should do a serious self-analysis of their management style to determine if they are micromanagers. This analysis could prevent a lot of unnecessary grief and aggravation.

Summary

CEOs of large organizations are typically compensated well for their efforts. However, that compensation comes with expectations…one of which is that these CEOs will make a limited number of mistakes.

This book focuses on the mistakes of CEOs in charge of large organizations. First, it discusses the importance of these CEOs. Next, it examines various indicators that determine their success. Last, and most importantly, it explores the mistakes these CEOs make and the impact those mistakes have on organizations.

Congratulations! You now understand more about CEO mistakes…which play a huge role in the growth and prosperity of organizations.

Consistently Inconsistent Leadership
Pros and Cons of a Surprisingly Popular Management Style

Introduction 36
- Lawsuits 36
- Demotivation 36
- Criticism 36
- Disrespect 37
- Barriers 37
- Commitment 37
- Motivation 37
- Praise 37
- Respect 37
- Communication 37

Pros and cons 38
- Goals and vision 38
- Sales and marketing 39
- Work and pleasure 39
- People and positions 40
- Growth and stability 41
- Inspiration and Innovation 41
- Customers and suppliers 42
- Changes and challenges 43

Future 44
Summary 45

Introduction

Good leaders do not all have the same management style. Some are hands-on while others are hands-off, some like the team concept while others prefer individualism, and some believe in a flat hierarchy structure while others prefer a rigid chain of command. However, regardless of preference, leaders use their chosen style to manage people and processes to accomplish organizational goals and objectives.

Typically, leaders who have experienced success with a particular management style will apply that style in all of their business encounters. They know that, based on experience, they will get what they need out of their people to get the job done. In other words, they are consistent in the way they manage their workforces.

There is nothing wrong with consistent management if it gets the job done. People might not like the chosen style of their leaders, but they have difficulty arguing against that style if it has been successful. However, some leaders choose to use multiple styles depending on the specifics of the situation. They do not manage with one particular technique, instead choosing to incorporate a variety of management styles to get the job done. This varied style of management is known as consistently inconsistent leadership (also known as CIL), and CIL is the focus of this book.

Sometimes it is important for those in leadership positions to remain consistent in their treatment of employees. For example, a manager should not tell an employee that she is doing well and then berate her an hour later. This type of behavior leads to misunderstanding about how the manager actually feels about the employee's work, and it prevents the employee from trusting her manager. This type of management behavior shows an abuse of CIL, and the results are negative.

When overused or abused, negatives of CIL include those listed below.

Lawsuits – This might be the most serious negative because it takes money and time to fight lawsuits and there is no guarantee of a victorious outcome. Ligation begins when employees perceive unfair treatment due to the uneven distribution of rules and policies…and uneven distribution of rules and policies is the foundation of CIL.

Demotivation – The opposite of motivation is demotivation, and demotivated employees are not as productive as those who are motivated to do their jobs. Managers who wrongly use CIL usually demotivate their employees because those employees do not like what they see. In some ways, demotivation is worse than anger because those employees choose to withdraw rather than fight…so their true feelings remain hidden.

Criticism – Nobody likes being criticized, and CIL can lead directly to criticism. Managers who wrongly use CIL open themselves up to attack from their subordinates, and those attacks can quickly spread through the workplace until the manager is thought of as a "loser" by the whole organization. Subordinate criticism might not hurt managers' feelings, but it might hurt their careers when it reaches the leaders of their organization. In short, their misuse of CIL can cost managers their jobs.

Disrespect – This refers to the respect that is lost when a manager overuses or abuses CIL. Employees lose respect for their bosses when they perceive favoritism or bias. They believe their bosses are well-aware of their actions, and the resulting disrespect puts up a wall that is difficult to tear down.

Barriers – This refers to the barriers that impede communication between employees and their supervisors. If overused or abused, CIL establishes a huge barrier to communication between workers and management. This barrier is strengthened as trust diminishes; thereby creating problems that are very difficult to resolve....even if CIS disappears completely.

The above negatives of CIL can be quite problematic for organizations. However, this does not mean CIL does not have good points. In fact, it is very beneficial when the problems of employees cannot be met with a "one size fits all" solution. In these situations, employees who get individualized attention feel like they are important to the organizations that employ them, and they react by doing things that help their employers achieve goals and objectives.

Interestingly, proper use of consistently inconsistent leadership has the exact opposite effect as overuse or abuse as shown below.

Commitment – Many employees find CIL works well for them because they personally benefit from this style of leadership. These workers are happy, and happy employees tend to be committed to the organizations that employ them. So, in the right situations, CIL helps organizations achieve goals and objectives because employee commitment is increased.

Motivation - CIL also helps motivate employees to do their best. Increased motivation, similar to increased commitment, is beneficial for helping organizations grow and prosper because goals are more easily achieved than they are in organizations with unmotivated employees.

Praise – Unfortunately, praise for management personnel in organizations is not very common. In fact, in most cases, they are criticized for their behavior rather than given accolades. CIL is one of the few management styles that leads to employees offering praise for managers and higher-up leaders because those employees feel they are being respected and treated fairly at work.

Respect - When properly used, CIL leads to higher levels of respect for the managers that use it. Essentially, this is positive payback from employees because they feel they are respected when their individual needs are addressed. The best thing about this mutual respect is that it creates a win/win situation for employees and organizations.

Communication – This refers to the opening up of communication due to the mutual respect that has transpired. CIL can open doors that were previously closed in management/employee relationships. When workers are happy, they want to communicate and share their everyday experiences with their bosses and leaders on the corporate ladder.

Essentially, managers need to know when to use CIL and when to use other management styles that are more rigid and structured. This starts by understanding employees and the jobs they are performing, which means hands-on leaders probably have an advantage over those who lead from a distance. In short, leaders who sit in an ivory tower are playing with fire if they manage their employees using a CIL style.

Many people are surprised to discover that CIL is a fairly common style of leadership. Astute leaders understand that all people are different and need individualized attention for motivation. This understanding, along with common sense and emotional intelligence, allows for the use of CIL techniques. However, some leaders also use CIL because they are inexperienced. They do not realize the potential problems that can result from employees' perception of unfair treatment, so they choose the CIL management style that has been shown to perpetuate inequity in workplaces.

Regardless of the reason for using CIL, it is the management style of choice for many people in leadership positions in a wide variety of industries and organizations. It is most common in small organizations because leaders can get to know their workers on a personal and professional basis. When they discover what motivates their employees, they custom tailor their management approach with them to get them to perform at high levels. For example, an owner of a retail store learns her jewelry department manager likes to fish. She brings this manager a set of fishing lures specially designed for catching trout. This motivates the manager to do his best for the owner because he believes she respects him.

The example above works well as a motivation tool for the jewelry department manager, but it could have a downside. If other managers find out about the lures given to the manager, then they might feel jealous or slighted because they did not receive any type of gift from the owner. If this happens, then the other managers could become demotivated due to the owner's inconsistent management of her employees.

So, this leads to a question. Should consistently inconsistent leadership be adopted by more managers to motivate employees and achieve organizational goals and objectives? Let's move forward to examine specific pros and cons of CIL so you can decide for yourself.

Pros and cons

Goals and vision

Goals are essentially stepping stones that work together to move organizations forward. They can be short-term or long-term, but all goals require employees to perform and progress toward a bigger idea….that idea being the vision of the organization.

Leaders set goals because those goals help employees focus on specific tasks while working toward the greater good of their organizations. This might sound rather cliché, but it is true. Employees need direction, and goals provide that direction. Employees also need motivation, and goals provide motivation through accomplishments. These accomplishments might be small, but they are significant because they break down organizational vision into smaller chunks that are easier to achieve than taking on the entire vision all at once.

Below are some pros and cons of consistently inconsistent management regarding goals and vision.

>*Pros* – Employees need to be motivated to achieve goals and perform at peak levels, and CIL provides that motivation.
>
>*Cons* – Employees who feel slighted because others have received rewards or accolades are likely to give up or pursue work elsewhere, and CIL is the culprit.

Consistently inconsistent leadership can help people be their best; thereby allowing the standards bar to be raised and improvement to be continuous. However, the standards bar will lower and improvement will cease if CIL leads to feelings of jealousy or wrongdoing.

Sales and marketing

Sales are critical to organizations worldwide because they generate the revenue necessary for survival and growth. Since salespeople and marketing personnel are responsible for generating sales, their importance cannot be underestimated. It is critical for companies to hire effective salespeople and marketing people…but that is often a much more challenging task than many people realize. In fact, some companies have "revolving doors" for these employees. New people are continually hired, but they are terminated or leave the organization in relatively short periods of time because they cannot meet the sales expectations set before them. In short, they might not be the right type of people for the jobs they are hired to perform.

Below are some pros and cons of consistently inconsistent management regarding sales and marketing.

>*Pros* – Some salespeople and marketing personnel become assertive and persistent because they have been catered to in terms of personal needs. In short, they are given the confidence needed to do their jobs to the best of their ability.
>
>*Cons* - Some salespeople and marketing personnel become aggressive and pushy because they have been catered to in terms of personal needs. In short, they develop arrogance and greed because the special attention has "gone to their heads."

Sales and marketing are critical for organizations. Without marketing, products and services do not become known to consumers. Without sales, there is no generation of revenue. CIL can help employees market and sell products because those employees feel good about themselves. However, CIL must be used with discretion because overconfidence can result in problems that are difficult to resolve.

Work and pleasure

Essentially, work and pleasure refer to the ability to accomplish work-related goals while enjoying life outside of work…commonly referred to as work-life balance. As people's lives get more hectic, they begin to realize the importance of work-life balance. Time is limited, and different things need to take priority at different times in life. People need to work to sustain a certain lifestyle, but they also need the time to enjoy that lifestyle.

Technology has completely changed work-life balance. People can now work and communicate with others from just about anywhere in the world. This means employees do not have to physically be at work to perform certain aspects of their jobs because they can telecommute. However, people need to understand that absolute work-life balance is unrealistic. The goal is to find a balance that works most of the time...and that balance might need to be tweaked periodically to adjust for changes in life or priorities.

Below are some pros and cons of consistently inconsistent management regarding work and pleasure.

> *Pros* – Everyone's definition of work-life balance is different. Some employees want time alone while others want time to travel with friends or visit with family. CIL gives managers the ability to customize solutions for their employees' individual needs.
>
> *Cons* – CIL can lead to employees taking advantage of the situation for their own personal gain rather than for the good of themselves and the organizations. In other words, they use CIL to Increase their personal time away from work and decrease their time working.

There must be a balance of work and pleasure for employees to find happiness at home and on the job. Consistently inconsistent leadership can work wonders for providing that balance if it is used properly. However, improper use of CIL can lead to greed and productivity issues that spiral out of hand.

People and positions

Processes and procedures dictate how people do their jobs, and sometimes the rules involved make it difficult for employees to find the creativity necessary to take ownership of the tasks they are performing. That ownership is critical because it empowers employees to perform to the best of their ability and, ultimately, accomplish the goals and objectives of their organizations.

CIL. when properly implemented, helps employees find creativity in somewhat restrictive environments. It does not necessarily break processing and procedural rules, but it bends them so employees become empowered and strive to do their best. In short, CIL helps employees become individuals in ways that are not possible when rigid command structures are in place.

It is rather obvious that consistently inconsistent leadership affects people because it intends to motivate people to do their best. Quite simply, it is a compliance gaining strategy put in place to get employees to achieve organizational goals and objectives. However, how does CIL affect positions? The answer is because people occupy those positions. Positions are nothing more than titles on paper until people fulfill the job responsibilities. Employees must be inspired to meet the challenges of their responsibilities, and that inspiration stems from the management styles of their leaders.

CIL inspires people to complete their job responsibilities because they have faith in their leaders. When employees like the way they are treated as individuals, they believe in the management system and work hard to give back to their organizations. In this sense, one hand washes the other.

Below are some pros and cons of consistently inconsistent management regarding people and positions.

> Pros – CIL helps employees trust leadership and buy into the management philosophy as a whole. When they believe in the leaders of their organizations, they make a conscious effort to accomplish the goals and objectives set forth by those leaders.

> Cons – When overused or misused, CIL can lead to mistrust of management. Once that trust is gone, it is difficult to re-establish.

Growth and stability

Growth and stability often go hand-in-hand as they help organizations evolve in a repetitive cycle. This might seem confusing, so it is more easily understood by remembering the following:

> *Growth creates stability and stability enables growth*

In progressive organizations, the above cycle repeats itself over and over; thereby allowing those organizations to raise the bar on expectations and achievements. All management styles affect this cycle, but few are more persuasive than consistently inconsistent leadership. CIL has a huge impact on the cycle because it takes into account individual needs to get the most out of people. Quite simply, it is a management style that is based on the assumption that people who are helped will return the favor in terms of their motivation, commitment, and performance.

Below are some pros and cons of consistently inconsistent management regarding growth and stability.

> *Pros* - CIL provides the spark that lights the fire for one hand washing the other. If employees feel they are being properly attended to, then they will reciprocate with the same treatment...which leads to organizational growth and stability.

> *Cons* - In terms of growth and stability, the biggest negative of CIL is misuse. If misused, CIL can have the exact opposite effect as that desired. In short, employees who perceive unfair treatment of others will hinder growth and stability due to negative attitudes.

Inspiration and Innovation

As has been said by many people in the past, innovation is one percent inspiration and ninety-nine percent perspiration. This statement might be true in many instances, but CIL has the potential to reverse the ratio by making it ninety-nine percent inspiration and one percent perspiration. This ratio changes because when workers' needs are met, they are naturally inspired to give back to their organizations. Many times this giving back is in the form of innovation.

Innovation stemming from CIL is typically not note-worthy or mind-boggling. It is made up of simple ideas that make people's jobs easier; thereby enhancing the productivity of the organization as a whole. However, regardless of the magnitude, innovative actions combine to create new concepts and ideas that help organizations grow and prosper.

Below are some pros and cons of consistently inconsistent management regarding inspiration and innovation.

> Pros - When used properly, CIL motivate employees to do their best. They readily take on new challenges and aspire to reach levels that they have previously not achieved. Many times their achievements stem from innovative thoughts and actions that facilitate processes, simplify tasks, and allow for greater productivity.

> Cons - Improperly used CIL can actually demotivate rather than inspire employees due to the perceived workplace inequities. If this happens, then innovation is unlikely as workers withdraw and do the minimum to get by.

Customers and suppliers

Most people understand that relationships with customers are critical because those customers provide the revenue necessary for organizations to function. However, people sometimes fail to realize the importance of relationships with suppliers. Without those suppliers, products cannot be built and services cannot be offered...so it is best to treat them with respect for their services.

It might seem hard to believe the internal management of employees affects their relationship with people on the outside. After all, what happens on the inside stays on the inside, and outsiders have their own unique set of problems that result from dealing with their own leaders. However, most employees realize that their jobs expand beyond their own workplaces into the organizations that supply them with raw materials and the organizations that purchase their finished products and services. This realization motivates them to work hard at maintaining positive relationships with customers and suppliers.

Below are some pros and cons of consistently inconsistent management regarding customers and suppliers.

> Pros - CIL builds external relationships because employees are motivated to perform to the best of their abilities and build bridges with everyone including customers and suppliers. This bridge-building is the result of positive attitudes due to individualized attention.

Cons - If used improperly or excessively, CIL can break down relationships with customers and suppliers due to the impact it has internally and externally. This is due to negative attitudes that result from perceived unfair treatment by management.

Changes and challenges

The pros and cons of changes and challenges are saved for last because every organization is challenged and every organization undergoes change. Interestingly, a challenge can lead to a change or a change can lead to a challenge. However, regardless of their relationship, changes and challenges play a huge role in the growth and development of organizations.

Change is critical for organizations because they will eventually need to undergo it or risk losing their ability to compete...which could lead to their inability to exist. All employees should accept change because their jobs might depend on it. However, this is typically not the case. In fact, many workers dislike change so much that they avoid it, ignore it, or fight it. On rare occasions these defense strategies are successful, but most of the time the change is going to happen, so it is best to embrace it.

Customer demands are possibly the most important reason for change because they are essential for survival. Customers want new products and services, and this requires organizations to do things differently. Competition is fierce as the global marketplace expands, and organizations that refuse to change lose the ability to be competitive. Once customers are gone, they might not return because other organizations are readily available to service their needs. If this happens, then any future attempt to change and make amends will be futile.

Technological advances also impact change. Virtually every organization in the world has been affected by technology. It makes many different work-related tasks faster and easier, and it brings products and services to market at record-breaking speed.

Technology has been great for productivity, but it also has some downsides. For example, it makes employees' jobs more complicated because they need to deal with so many other variables. Cell phones and email have resulted in people expecting immediate answers to their questions and concerns, and this adds pressure and stress to workforces with limited time and human resources. However, regardless of the positive or negative effects of technology, it requires employees to change. If they do not change, they will not keep up with the competition...and this can lead to the downfall of their organizations.

Most people who have worked for any type of organization realize that change is difficult for many employees. This is due to the challenges that are created, such as fear of the unknown. People do not like to leave their established comfort zones because they do not know what will happen. They are leaving familiar surroundings to venture into the unknown, and this makes them apprehensive.

Fear of job loss is another challenge in getting employees to accept change. Change often occurs because it makes processes and procedures more efficient. This is especially true for technological change. However, the downside to technological change is that it can eliminate jobs. Employees are aware of this threat, and they sometimes become a barrier to change because of it.

The last challenge for the implementation of change involves leadership. Management needs to support the change from start to finish, and this is not always the case. Typically management understands that change needs to start at the top of the organizational hierarchy. However, some leaders fail to understand the importance of their involvement. They have a few meetings and pass on the responsibilities to lower-level managers. Yes, they were initially involved...but the rank and file employees are not aware of that involvement. The workers only see their supervisor telling them about the change that is about to take place.

Management needs to be continuously involved with change as it takes place, but they rarely do this. They typically implement the change and then move on to other job responsibilities. They completely remove themselves from the process and limit their involvement to occasional monitoring of the change progression. This plan of action does not work because it shows that management has no interest in seeing the change through. They are not dedicated to the overall process, and that lack of dedication trickles down to the rest of the employees.

Below are some pros and cons of consistently inconsistent management regarding changes and challenges.

> *Pros* - Managers must address the individual needs of their employees or those employees will not believe in the changes that are taking place. CIL works well for addressing worker needs and, in some situations, change cannot happen without it.

> *Cons* - CIL can backfire if used excessively during change because employees expect this leadership style to be used during all of their challenges. There are situations, such as an increase in the health insurance co-pay of workers, where CIL is not practical and "one size fits all" management must be employed.

Changes and challenges are difficult for employees, but CIL can reduce that difficulty by showing concern for individual needs. However, CIL is not a "catch-all" solution to all issues related to changes and challenges; thereby causing some employees to develop negative perceptions of their workplaces based on their expectations of management style.

Future

Before moving into a prediction of the future, it is important to note that many leadership purists disdain any form of consistently inconsistent leadership. This hatred is based on the thinking that uneven treatment of employees creates the risk that more problems will result, and, at some point, those problems will not be resolvable. The possibility of more problems is a reality, but there is also a potential upside where employees feel appreciated and empowered to do their best...which is why the future of CIL is important to discuss.

The future of anything is difficult, if not impossible, to accurately predict due to the factors involved and the variables that can change. However, basic management styles have remained fairly consistent over the years while gaining or losing popularity as new generations of leaders take over the reins of organizations. Based on the past history of these styles, it can be said with relative confidence that, in some form, they will be around and used by leaders in the future.

Consistently inconsistent management plays a role in many different aspects of leadership, and it has the potential to be beneficial or destructive to people and workplaces. The potential positives and negatives of CIL make it a risky management style. but, regardless of the risks, it will be around as long as organizations exist.

So, like it or not, consistently inconsistent communication will be here in the long run. It is not going away and it could possibly increase in popularity, especially if the job market is tight and employees are difficult to find, hire, and keep. When markets are tight, leaders will gamble with the styles they use to manage employees...and CIL is one of those styles that has the potential to pay off in big ways.

Summary

People who use consistently inconsistent leadership to manage others are taking a risk because it can help organizations grow and prosper or it can put those organizations on the brink of disaster. However, the risk involved will not deter managers from using CIL because of its potential for being beneficial. It was used in the past, it is used now, and it will be used in the future...regardless of the naysayers who despise it.

This book focuses on consistently inconsistent management by introducing the subject matter, examining its pros and cons in specific situations, and predicting its future. The text is informational and educational, and it is written for easy understanding at all reader levels. Hopefully, you learned something as you progressed through the various sections.

Congratulations! You now understand more about consistently inconsistent management...a leadership style that is more common than many people realize.

Coworker Relationships
in Organizations
Establishing, Maintaining, and Improving

Introduction
Openness to experience 48
Conscientiousness 48
Extraversion 49
Agreeableness 49
Neuroticism 49

Strategy
. . . . 50
Apply Industrial/Organizational Psychology . . . 51
Keep discussions confidential 52
Monitor written words 53
Listen actively 54
Proceed with caution on social media 57
Use common courtesy 60

Summary
. . . . 61

Introduction

Employees in organizations typically spend a lot of time with their coworkers. In fact, barring those who travel extensively or work remotely, some employees spend more time with their coworkers than they do with their family and friends. When coworkers spend this much time together, disagreements of some type are unavoidable. These disagreements are not necessarily bad, but they need to be resolved or relationships start to dissolve and conflict becomes the norm. This conflict might be limited to personal interaction in the beginning, but it eventually crosses over the line into work-related activities; thereby hindering productivity for everyone involved....including the employees who had nothing to do with the disagreement that started everything.

Workplace disagreements often stem from differences in employees' personalities. Essentially, five basic dimensions make up the human personality. They include openness to experience, conscientiousness, extraversion, agreeableness, and neuroticism (conveniently remembered by the acronym OCEAN). These dimensions were first established by Ernest Tupes and Raymond Christal in 1961, but many other researchers focused and refined their findings to come up with what is commonly known as the "Big Five."

The following are simplified definitions of the big five dimensions of personality, along with a workplace example of each for further clarification:

Openness to experience

This refers to the extent to which people are adventurous, social, curious, and active. Imagination and creativity are preferred over a standard routine, and independence often plays a significant role. Artists and songwriters often have this dimension as part of their personalities.

> Linda is a tour guide in Africa who is originally from the United States. She likes adventure and travel so she moved to Africa to lead people on jungle tours through multiple nations. Her groups travel by boat, plane, bus, car, four-wheeler, and even elephant to get to remote areas of the wild and explore the terrain. The wild animals and local people encountered during the tours have caused some situations to become dangerous, but that danger just makes things more fun for Linda as she follows her passion.
>
> Linda has found her calling due to a personality that is truly open to experience.

Conscientiousness

This dimension alludes to reliability, responsibility, carefulness, and self-discipline. In some ways, this is the opposite of the openness to experience dimension. People high in conscientiousness include accountants and laboratory technicians.

> Samuel is a nurse who cares for prematurely born babies. His job involves monitoring the infant's vital signs, administering their medications, and observing them for health

issues that might require a doctor. His daily activities are very regulated and regimented.

Samuel does very well at his job because he is responsible, careful, and self-disciplined. He has a very conscientious personality.

Extraversion

This dimension makes up a personality that is assertive, energizing, excitable, and lively. People with high extraversion are typically outgoing and very involved in their pursuit of goals. This characterization is the opposite of an introverted personality where individuals prefer to keep to themselves. People high in extraversion include politicians and ministers.

Jalen is a college basketball coach. He is passionate about his job and gets personally involved with his players…he even participates in team scrimmages. Jalen's players like his style of coaching, and they think he is a great motivator.

Jalen has an energizing personality that is vividly displayed when he coaches the players on his basketball team.

Agreeableness

This dimension refers to kindness, consideration, generosity, and trustworthiness. Willingness to help others takes precedence over self-interests, and people are viewed optimistically. This is the opposite of disagreeableness where self-interest ranks above everything else. People high in agreeableness are often conflict avoiders in organizations.

Akira is from Japan. Respect is very important in his culture, so he will not argue with people at his job. He is not opposed to conflict, but he values harmony above any type of disagreement.

Akira's coworkers think he is very kind and considerate, and they respect him for his position on arguments. He has a personality that is high in agreeableness, and his resulting behavior reduces conflict in the workplace.

Neuroticism

Unpleasant emotions are a major part of this dimension. They include anger, anxiety, hopelessness, and depression. People high in neuroticism are often emotionally unstable, and they view minor setbacks very negatively…even to the point where they believe those setbacks are permanent issues with no resolution.

Janelle works as a waitress in a restaurant. She gets depressed when her customers do not tip the customary twenty percent. In fact, every time this happens, she cries and considers quitting her job because she believes she is not a good waitress.

Unfortunately, Janelle is emotionally unstable at work. She views minor setbacks as major problems, and they lead her into a state of hopelessness. Janelle is irrational and has a neurotic personality.

The above descriptions paint a picture of the big five dimensions that make up the human personality (remember the acronym OCEAN). These dimensions affect how people behave in many aspects of their jobs, and they can lead to disagreements that result in conflict.

Groups tend to take on a personality of their own after the members start to learn to work together, but they are affected by individual personalities. For example, consider a group situation in a workplace with an introvert and an extrovert as team members. The introverted person and extroverted person do not work towards accomplishing goals in the same manner, and one is not going to influence the other to change. The relationship between these two employees becomes worse as the group moves forward, as the example below illustrates.

> Cindy and Mitch are assigned to a team project that has a goal of reducing costs at their company by five percent. Cindy is a very organized accountant, and she is most comfortable using methodical step-by-step approaches to problem-solving. Mitch, who works in marketing, likes to experiment with new and different ways to solve problems...regardless of whether or not those methods have worked in the past.
>
> From the start, Mitch and Cindy argue about the direction of the team. Mitch views Cindy as boring and old-fashioned, and Cindy views Mitch as pompous and careless. This relationship gradually gets worse as the team moves forward, and soon personal attacks become part of their dialogue.
>
> After three weeks, no solutions for the desired cost reduction have been found. A vice president at the company is forced to scrap the team and start over with a new group of individuals who have more homogeneous personalities.

Due to clashing introvert and extrovert personalities, Mitch and Cindy's team was unable to progress and accomplish the objectives established by their employer. The productivity of the entire team was hindered due to the conflict that resulted from Mitch and Cindy's disagreements, and the end result probably would have been much different if they had a good working relationship.

Based on the potential for conflict hindering productivity, it is rather obvious that good coworker relationships are important in organizations. This book is written to help people understand and improve those relationships so everyone is able to perform at peak levels. Let's move on to the next section that discusses a strategy for establishing, maintaining, and improving coworker relationships.

Strategy

It is a well-known fact that good coworker relationships are critical for career advancement in the corporate world. Corporate leaders had to work with others to advance up the ladder, and the people they befriended supported them during their climb to the top. If they had alienated these people, then they would have kicked the ladder out from underneath them as they attempted to ascend. Quite simply, these leaders established and maintained good coworker relationships throughout their careers…and these relationships were paramount to their success.

The above paragraph leads to a question. What did these leaders do to establish and maintain good coworker relationships that others can use as they ascend in their own careers? The following provides answers to this question by highlighting the most important aspects of their relationship success while discussing how those relationships are established, maintained, and improved:

Apply Industrial/Organizational Psychology

Establishing and maintaining

Industrial/organizational (I/O) psychology is a branch of clinical psychology that focuses on workers and workplaces. Essentially, it applies science to organizations to find out what employees enjoy most about their jobs.

I/O psychologists study organizational behavior using established principles, practices, and theories from the field of psychology. They conduct research designed to improve employee attitudes through training and feedback from management. They also help employees transition into unfamiliar work environments as organizations grow, change, and evolve. Their goal is to improve various aspects of work-life including safety, mental health, job satisfaction, productivity, and motivation. In short, they strive to resolve workplace issues and improve the quality of life for employees.

Most employees are not I/O psychologists. This is not a problem because they do not need to be I/O psychologists to better their careers…they simply need to apply some of the basic principles. Social awareness is one of these principles. Workers who experience successful coworker relationships are aware of the reasons for their coworkers' behavior. They process information and learn from their experiences to understand why people react the way they do to workplace experiences. Without this skill, employees can wrongly analyze situations and make inaccurate conclusions; thereby leading to disagreements and conflict in organizations. It takes time and effort to master social awareness, but the payback is worth that time and effort because it makes people better at their jobs.

Learning is another I/O psychology skill that employees can use to form good relationships with their coworkers. Every worker needs to learn something about his or her job to get better at it, and part of this learning requires the involvement of others. Successful employees reach out and show interest in the job tasks their coworkers perform, and this interest starts the bonding process. Once the bonding begins, a trust develops that can be expanded upon with just about any conversation to maintain a good working relationship.

Improving

You should periodically act as a sounding board for your coworkers. Employees like to bounce thoughts, ideas, and problems off others, and listening to them lets them know that you care about them personally. If your coworkers know you will listen to them, then they will naturally want to form a closer relationship with you.

Also, remember to follow up on conversations. If a problem was discussed, then ask if it was resolved in a future conversation. If you never mention that problem again, then you will be viewed as uncaring or not listening to what they had to say. Most employees like to talk about their work concerns, and they will gravitate toward you if you show interest...now and in the future.

Keep discussions confidential

Establishing and maintaining

Most states have laws in place that protect confidential information such as social security numbers, banking information, health-related documents, and legal transactions. However, this section is not referring to this kind of confidential information because the rules are clear and there are penalties for allowing it to get into the wrong hands. Confidentiality in this section refers to daily discussions among coworkers that are not protected by the law and might or might not be work-related. There are no written rules or procedures in place for exposure of these discussions, but there are unwritten protocols that many people expect will be followed...or their trust will be violated.

Confidentiality is very important to some people. In fact, some individuals place such a high value on it that they will not talk to people who lack the ability to keep things confidential. This is particularly true in organizations where, in addition to being embarrassed, people's reputations and careers could suffer if their conversation is shared with the workforce. For these reasons, people who cannot keep secrets are disliked by their coworkers while those who maintain confidentiality form bonds that help establish good working relationships.

Improving

It should be easy to keep discussions with coworkers confidential because all you have to do is avoid telling others about those discussions. If you do not talk about the subject matter, then you will not have to decide if you are releasing confidential information because people will never know the discussion existed. More importantly, those same people will not ask questions that press you for more information that should not be divulged. That being said, the best advice for keeping discussions with coworkers confidential is to practice keeping your mouth shut. This can be challenging at first, but it gets easier to do over time because you will see the benefits.

Keeping your mouth shut works well for confidentiality purposes, but this type of action (or non-action) takes place after the discussions are over. There are also ways to improve the quality of these discussions as they transpire. Let coworkers vent while you listen attentively. Your fellow workers experience many different types of frustration at their jobs, and sometimes they want to tell you about that frustration. When you listen to venting coworkers, you establish bonds with them because they feel like they are being heard without worrying about their comments being leaked to other employees.

So, in a nutshell, when coworkers discuss something confidential with you, do not relay that information to others to avoid the possibility of those coworkers losing trust in you and damaging your relationship with them.

Monitor written words

Establishing and maintaining

Written words are sometimes more important than spoken words because they lack non-verbal communication for clarity. Humor, sarcasm, hand gestures, head nodding, and body position all influence communication during face-to-face interaction. With the exception of emoticons, these influences are usually not part of writing. Additionally, written words can be confusing when the reader does not understand how a word is emphasized. For example, consider the phrase, "thank you for making my day." This could be a true heart-felt thank you, an attempt at humor, or a form of sarcasm. Although this phrase is written properly, it can be misconstrued by those reading it.

The written word can easily damage relationships with coworkers if the meaning is distorted or misinterpreted. People who are offended often stay offended and will not talk to the person who wrote the message. The worst part about this is the offended people might remain silent, so the offender will never know he or she did anything wrong. To prevent relationship damage, it is imperative to write clearly and effectively. This is not easy, but it can be done with a little patience, time, and effort.

Improving

You need to be able to write effectively or you risk losing the intent of your messages. For example, consider the following sentence:

> Robert never said Katie stole your cell phone.

Now notice how the meaning changes each time the sentence is read, but a different word is emphasized (the emphasized word is capitalized):

- ROBERT never said Katie stole your cell phone (meaning Robert did not say Katie stole your cell phone, but another person may have said she stole it)
- Robert NEVER said Katie stole your cell phone (meaning Robert did not say Katie stole your cell phone at all)
- Robert never SAID Katie stole your cell phone (meaning Robert did not say Katie stole your cell phone, but he implied it)
- Robert never said KATIE stole your cell phone (meaning Robert did not say Katie stole your cell phone, but he did say someone else stole it)
- Robert never said Katie STOLE your cell phone (meaning Robert did not say Katie stole your cell phone, but she borrowed it)

- Robert never said Katie stole YOUR cell phone (meaning Robert did not say Katie stole your cell phone, but she stole another person's cell phone)
- Robert never said Katie stole your CELL PHONE (meaning Robert did not say Katie stole your cell phone, but she stole something of yours other than your cell phone)

The above sentence shows how words do not always convey the intended message. People who misinterpret the word emphasis of your message change the context and distort your intended meaning. You need to write clearly so there is no room for distortion. For example, the above sentence is re-written below for better understanding and maximum clarity.

> Nobody said or implied that anyone stole or borrowed anything that belonged to somebody else.

If you write the sentence as above, then everyone reading it will understand the intent of the message. They will understand what you are trying to communicate to them, and this makes their jobs easier. They will also find you pleasurable to work with; thereby strengthening your relationships with them.

The key takeaway from the example above is to think about written messages before you send them, and then adjust the wording to reflect your thoughts. If you write effectively, people will like you more because they will understand what you are saying.

Listen actively

Establishing and maintaining

Listening plays a big role in communication. In fact, it might be the most important aspect of communication because lack of it tends to create a wealth of misunderstandings.

Listening is a process that involves focusing on what someone else is saying. On the surface, this might seem like an easy task...but that is typically not the case due to the barriers that are present. These barriers include noise, visual distractions, emotions, fatigue, anger, accents, language, jargon, and acronyms. All of these barriers lead to misunderstanding because the message that is being sent is not comprehended.

The previous paragraph makes it seem like listening is a lost cause because it has so many barriers. Fortunately, this is not true. With a little concentration, it is possible to hear and comprehend what is being said by others. This is good because effective listening has many benefits including:

> **Understanding** - There is no doubt that effective listening creates a better understanding of the discussion that is transpiring. Without understanding, most conversations are severely hindered. Think about holding a conversation with a friend inside a crowded bar that has loud music playing. The loud music and crowd noise create a barrier to effective listening, and the resulting lack of understanding hinders the conversation.
>
> **Efficiency** - When people listen to each other, everything becomes more efficient. They understand what is being said, and this results in less confusion and mistakes. In this sense, it is much easier to accomplish goals and tasks that are a part of everyday life.
>
> **Insight** - When people hear what is actually being said, they gather information that can be used to defend their positions and make decisions. This information influences behavior and brings about change that helps individuals reach the mindset where they feel the most comfortable. People who do not effectively listen fail to acquire information, and they are often left uncertain of the direction they need to take on important aspects of the conversation. In short, people who listen effectively gain insight that benefits them.
>
> **Bonding** - This is likely the least known benefit of effective listening, but often it is the most important of those listed in this book. This is because trust builds when one person believes another is listening to them. ..and trust leads to bonding.

Conversations are also more enjoyable when effective listening is employed because there is less repeating of what has already been said. In this regard, effective listing helps people bond because speakers believe their words are important and not easily forgotten. They do not get annoyed from being asked to repeat the words that they have just spoken, and this prevents the potential conflict that can occur when people become upset with others for an apparent lack of interest or concern.

Obviously, listening is important. That being said, most people can stand to improve in this area...and that improvement comes in the form of active listening. Active listening means fully concentrating on the speaker while blocking out all distractions. This is a learned skill that takes work, but it can be achieved with some time and effort.

Improving

Something known as the listening ladder can help you become more of an active listener. LADDER is an acronym that helps with active listening. It has been around for many years and it is often used by consultants to help people improve their listening skills. LADDER stands for the following:

> **L - Look at the person talking to you** - People who look away from the speaker appear uninterested or bored. When this happens, speakers tend to shut down because they feel that they are not getting the proper attention paid to them. Some speakers even become upset because they feel insulted, so you should look at them.
>
>> **Note:** When listening on the telephone, the "L" may stand for limit doing other things such as typing, writing, using a calculator, trying to hold another conversation, or attempting to answer another call. You might prefer to perform multiple tasks, but often times a telephone conversation deserves your complete attention.

A - Ask questions - Follow-up questions need to be asked to fully comprehend what the speaker is saying. These questions should be open-ended so explanation and expansion of the subject matter are possible. For example, rather than asking a woman if she likes her job, you should ask to ask her to explain what she likes and dislikes about her job. A simple yes or no does not always give enough information…just ask anyone who has been through a legal deposition.

D – Don't change the subject - Changing the subject is a very common mistake that people make when they are supposed to be listening. For example, a speaker is talking about the beautiful rivers she saw during a recent trip to Alaska, and you change the subject to the beautiful Everglades you saw during a trip to Florida. The woman feels as if the spotlight has shifted from her trip to your vacation…and this is frustrating.

D – Don't interrupt - Some people tend to interrupt others when they are speaking. Instead of listening, these individuals are thinking about what they are going to say next…and this interferes with their comprehension of what the speaker is saying. Interruption is sometimes necessary for clarification purposes, but you should avoid it as a general rule.

E - Emotions…control emotions - Not surprisingly, emotions should be controlled when listening to someone speak. Outbursts should be avoided because they prevent effective listening and lead to other problems such as disagreement or conflict.

R - Respond to the person speaking - Listeners who engage themselves will listen more effectively because they are involved in the conversation. Fortunately, engagement can be accomplished without asking questions or interrupting. For example, you can smile, nod your head, raise your eyebrows, or lean forward to show interest. Additionally, simple phrases such as "I understand" or "that makes sense" can also be used as response techniques.

Active listening shows you are listening to what others have to say by taking the time to understand what they really mean. Ask questions for clarification, avoid finishing sentences, and prevent yourself from interrupting if you truly want to understand the key points others are making. Active listening is an acquired skill, and you need to make that acquisition to help improve coworker relationships.

Proceed with caution on social media

Establishing and maintaining

Social media is a major vehicle for the transmission of electronic communication all over the world. It is computer-mediated communication dedicated to collaboration, content-sharing, and interaction. It is a method of sharing information for people and organizations, and it is growing in popularity. In fact, many people believe that social media as we know it today is in its infancy due to technology that has not yet been discovered. When that technology is discovered, the social media we know now might look like rotary-dial landline phones of the past.

The number of social media categories is often debated due to the overlap and specific types involved. For example, media sharing is sometimes broken into subcategories of pictures, videos, and live-streaming videos. However, for the generalization purposes of this book, media sharing encompasses all of these subcategories.

Social media categories for organizations are listed below.

> **Social Networking** - Sometimes referred to as relationship networks, social networks allow people to share a wealth of information about who they are and what they do. These communication channels reach people all over the world with a few clicks of a mouse. As most people are aware, Facebook is the major social network with over a billion users. However, LinkedIn is very popular with organizations because it is geared to the business community.
>
> **Microblogging** - This category of social media shares information in short messages. When people microblog, they do not have to worry about sending out "spam" type messages or losing the interest of followers due to information overload. However, the information that can be sent is very limited...sometimes to the point where it is ineffective. Twitter is a very popular form of microblogging that is even used by Donald Trump.
>
> **Blogging** - Blogging is social media that allows much more detail than microblogging...and that is why it deserves its own category. It works great for keeping people in the public eye. Other advantages of blogging are that it helps companies promote their other forms of social media and, in terms of marketing, it drives brands and images. Word press might be the most popular blogging platform because it is relatively easy to use and can be custom designed for any person or organization.
>
> **Social News** - Social news is similar to social networking because it shares news and information with followers. However, social news specializes in allowing readers to cast votes to determine which news or information is displayed the most prominently. People benefit from this platform when they are liked and displayed based on voter preferences. Digg is a popular social news site that has promoted a wide variety of products and services offered by companies.
>
> **Media Sharing** - If a picture is worth a thousand words, then media sharing is 1000 times more powerful than writing-based social media. It is essentially the

sharing of photographs, video, and live-streaming video. People and organizations can benefit from media sharing by promoting their workplaces, products, or services. Flickr is a popular image site, YouTube is well-known for videos, and Periscope is routinely used for live-streaming videos.

Online reviews - Online reviews are popular now, and their popularity is continuing to grow. Consumers want to know more about the products and services they purchase, and online reviews provide information that helps them obtain that knowledge. This category of social media allows people to rate a company, product, or service…and then discuss why they gave it that rating. Yelp is a well-known online review service that impacts a wide variety of businesses.

E-commerce - This category of social media works well for businesses (typically retailers) because many people prefer the ease of buying products online. It allows people to view and purchase goods and services from a variety of different retailers with the click of a button. E-commerce gives companies the ability to upload images of their products and services that link back to their websites or product pages. Pinterest and Amazon have E-commerce capabilities, but Polyvore is an actual example of E-commerce that has become quite popular.

Content Curation - This category is somewhat similar to social news and social networking because it shares information. However, there is no voting or discussion between followers. Organizations find content curation valuable because it gives them exposure and can generate the interest of potential customers. A good example of this social media category is Wikipedia; a site that is maintained by its users.

Social networking and blogging are probably the two most common categories of social media used by individuals because they are great for reaching many people at the same time. However, this kind of exposure also has a downside. It can do damage to people and their relationships with others…and sometimes those others are their coworkers. Employees who expose information about themselves or others can look bad in the eyes of their coworkers. This is why those who exercise caution on social media often form strong working relationships.

Improving

The best advice for improving coworker relationships via social media is "when in doubt, throw it out." In other words, if the content has the potential to offend someone, then do not post or upload it. This applies when you post or upload things about yourself or others because either way, it could upset someone even though it does not offend you.

Unfortunately, it is much easier for you to post comments on a computer than it is to say those same words during face-to-face interaction with other employees. For this reason, you should assume that the content you post or upload is read or viewed by all of your coworkers. Think about how your comments, pictures, jokes, political viewpoints, religious beliefs, etc. might offend specific people, and you will be less likely to upload things that negatively impact your coworker relationships.

Use common courtesy

Establishing and maintaining

When people are young, they are often told by their elders, "treat people the way you want to be treated." This advice has great application throughout life…regardless of whether that application is personal or professional. However, employees in workplaces often need to see each other regularly, and poor relationships between them are sure to hinder their productivity. As might be expected, poor relationships develop when people feel like they are not being treated with the same consideration, politeness, and respect that they give others.

Essentially, treating others with consideration, politeness, and respect is accomplished using common courtesy. Common courtesy involves things as simple as saying "hello" or "thank you," and it should be done consistently to maintain good coworker relationships. For example, if you said "good morning" to a coworker yesterday, then this does not exempt you from saying the same today….and every morning in the future. Along the same lines, thanking people for their help shows respect and that same respect should be shown in the future when help is provided.

Improving

Below are some suggestions for extending common courtesy in workplaces:

> **Avoid complaining** - As noted earlier in this book, everyone likes to vent about their problems. However, this venting can become outright annoying if it is constant…and it will cause people to avoid you. When people avoid you, you cannot establish good relationships with them. In short, limit your complaining and people will like you much more than those who gripe about everything.
>
> **Respect time** – In organizations, time is important because there are limited work hours in the day. For this reason, common courtesy includes respecting others' time. Employees who monopolize their coworkers' time are often disliked because their coworkers have other tasks they need to complete. You need to understand this and give people time to do what they need to do…or they will begin to avoid you. If you are avoided, you will not develop good working relationships with others, and you will pay the price on your job.
>
> **Collaborate** – Collaboration involves working with others to exchange ideas and complete job tasks. Collaboration also makes coworker relationships important to obtain information. Unfortunately, some employees do not reach out to others for assistance because they do not think they need their help. They would rather do things alone, but sometimes this is simply not possible. When

they need the help of others, that help is not available because they have not developed the bonding necessary to get it.

Do not put yourself in a position where you cannot get help from your coworkers. Reach out to them by putting out a "welcome mat" for their thinking. Then practice common courtesy during collaboration by giving them credit for their ideas, praising them for the information they share, and helping them achieve more by providing your thoughts and ideas. This type of behavior goes a long way toward building relationships and getting the help you require when you need it.

Avoid being "that jerk" - This applies more to personal aspects of employees' behavior in workplaces, but it does affect relationships. You need to avoid being the person who always or never does something. For example, you do not want to be "that jerk" who always leaves a mess for others to clean up, or "that jerk" who never makes another pot of coffee after you take the last cup. Some employees do not take this type of improvement seriously, and they jeopardize their relationships with coworkers. Do not be like those employees and choose to build bridges rather than walls with your coworkers. Do the little things that make them happy so they welcome your presence and desire to talk to you. This will help you form relationships on a personal and professional level.

Avoid gossip and rumors

This suggestion is saved for last because rumors and gossip can destroy coworker relationships very quickly...and, unfortunately, some of those relationships cannot be repaired. Start by keeping an open mind by not always believing what you hear. Do not participate by furthering gossip or rumors, and keep a close watch on what you tell others about the things you have heard. This will help prevent damage to the relationships you have with the workers being talked about. Additionally, if you believe a rumor could be true, then assume a mistake was made and move forward. For example, you hear that an IT employee made a mistake that caused part of the server to be hijacked. You might believe that this mistake occurred, but forgive the IT person for his error. This will help prevent you from wanting to discuss the matter with others. It will also help you avoid a potentially ugly situation that could take place if the IT person finds out you are saying bad things about his work performance. In this example, gossip is not good for you because it could destroy your chance of having a good working relationship with the IT employee.

Summary

Good coworker relationships in workplaces are very beneficial because they encourage collaboration, build morale, inspire creativity, and increase productivity. Without good relationships, employees are not able to perform at optimum levels, and they can be viewed as liabilities rather than assets in their organizations.

This book focuses on coworker relationships in organizations. It discusses the benefits of these relationships and suggests methods for maintaining and improving them. The text is educational and informational, and it is written for easy reader understanding at all levels.

Congratulations! You now understand more about establishing, maintaining, and improving coworker relationships...all of which are important in workplaces all over the world.

Delegation in Organizations
Understanding, Exemplifying, and Improving

Introduction   65
Reasons to delegate   65
    Productivity   65
    Commitment   66
    Education   66
    Efficiency   67

Reasons not to delegate   68
    Laziness   68
    Power   68
    Qualifications   69
    Responsibility   69

Delegation strategy   70
    Match expertise   70
    Explain reasoning   70
    Define responsibilities   71
    Encourage participation   71
    Follow up   71
    Provide feedback   71

Improving delegation   72
    Avoid micromanaging   72
    Delegate uniformly   73
    Provide resources   74
    Identify goals   74

Summary   74

Introduction

What exactly is delegation? It is similar to empowerment because lower-ranking employees are given the power to make decisions. However, it differs from empowerment because employees who are delegated tasks are not completely responsible for the successful completion of those tasks. Some of the responsibility rests on the people who did the delegating.

All good leaders delegate effectively. At first glance, this might appear to be a rather bold statement. After all, many leaders do not delegate effectively and this causes a variety of problems within their organizations. However, the keyword in the first sentence of this paragraph is "good." All leaders are not good leaders because good leaders delegate effectively.

Reasons to delegate

Delegation is often the key to the success of an organization. When managers delegate, they relieve some of their workloads, and this allows them to focus on other tasks. Additionally, those on the receiving end of the delegation become more interested in work because their jobs are more challenging.

The following are other reasons why delegation is important in organizations:

Productivity

When work is delegated, productivity increases. This is because work is broken down into manageable portions that are given to different employees. Psychologically, this is easier than handling an entire project because people are not faced with an overwhelming amount of work that needs to be finished. They see a small of work, and this inspires them to get it done.

When employees complete their portion of the job, they give it back to the delegating individual and are ready to move on to their next assignment. Ultimately, work gets completed in a timelier manner and productivity improves.

Organizational example

Geraldine is an inventory control manager at a national pet food distributor. She has been assigned the job of categorizing each type of pet food by animal (dog, cat, bird, rabbit, horse, etc.) and food type (dry, moist, liquid, grain, pellet, etc.).

This project is large-scale and complex due to the 4000 items inventoried at the pet food distributor. Geraldine would be overwhelmed if she attempted to complete the job alone, so she has decided to delegate the work to three employees in her department. Ronald has been assigned farm animals (horses, goats, pigs, chickens, etc.), Jenny has been assigned common household animals (dogs, cats, ferrets, fish, etc.), and Michelle has been assigned exotic animals (monkeys, snakes, alligators, cougars, etc.).

Each employee views their work as something that they can complete. Within one week, they have all finished their assignments. The categorized lists are entered into the computer, and Geraldine adds finishing touches to complete the project.

If Geraldine had tried to take on this project by herself, she estimated it would have taken her at least six weeks. By delegating the work, the total time needed was only about half of that estimate. In short, delegation substantially increased productivity at the pet food distributor because the work was broken into manageable portions.

Commitment

As noted earlier, delegation is similar to empowerment because employees are given decision-making power. This power results in employees taking responsibility for the jobs they are performing, and that responsibility commits them to the goals and objectives of the organization.

Organizational example

> Bertram is a condominium manager for a company that owns and operates apartment and condominium complexes all over the United States. The company has made safety of the residents a major priority, and they stress that priority in meetings, letters, and emails.
>
> The residents in Bertram's complex are constantly losing keys to the common areas (pool, community center, exercise room, etc.). This is a safety concern because unauthorized people could find the keys and enter the buildings. Bertram's boss at corporate headquarters has delegated him the task of implementing a different type of security system in the common areas that does not require keys.
>
> Bertram takes his assignment seriously. He feels responsible and wants the job done right, so he diligently researches his options using the internet and his local suppliers. Ultimately, he chooses an entry system that recognizes the thumbprints of the residents. This prevents unauthorized people from entering the common areas, and the residents cannot lose keys.
>
> This system works well, and Bertram is proud of his accomplishment. How he constantly searches for new ways to make the condominium complex safer for the residents. In short, Bertram feels personally committed to the safety goals of his organization.

Education

One of the best things about delegation is that it allows employees to learn. They are assigned a task, and they are responsible for following that task through to completion. This takes time and effort, but it also provides a real-world learning experience that cannot be obtained by reading a book or sitting in a classroom.

Organizational example

Lola is the head librarian at the main branch of a college library. Her boss has given her the task of setting up a coffee shop in the library where students can purchase food and beverages.

Lola is a bit apprehensive because she has never set up a coffee shop, but she is excited about the opportunity and immediately gets started. She spends many hours contacting and meeting with vendors for help on this project and is sometimes confused about the direction she needs to take. However, after a few months, the coffee shop is up and running due to her hard work and effort.

Lola now understands what it is like to do something entirely different than what she has ever done in the past. She was forced to move outside her comfort zone and struggled at times, but she was ultimately successful.

Lola learned a lot from this experience, and it gave her the confidence to move on to other tasks outside of her area of expertise. She was challenged by the delegation she received from her boss….but it paid dividends in terms of education.

Efficiency

Organizations operate more efficiently when work is delegated because jobs can be matched with employees' skills. This allows delegators to break down specific aspects of jobs by expertise. For example, cost aspects can be delegated to accountants, specification aspects can be delegated to quality assurance people, architectural aspects can be delegated to engineers, and training aspects can be delegated to human resources personnel.

Organizational example

Samuel works at a rubber manufacturing company as a manager of the chemistry laboratory. In this capacity, he oversees the laboratory and four chemists.

Samuel's boss is Carrie, the vice president of operations. Carrie is working on a project that involves a more durable type of rubber designed for race car tires. She needs to manufacture this product using specified materials at a pre-determined cost on existing equipment.

Carrie delegates specific areas of this project as follows:

- The cost requirements are delegated to the accounting manager.
- The production requirements are delegated to the plant manager.
- The technical requirements are delegated to Samuel.

Carrie's delegation makes sense because each area of the project is delegated to the employee with the most expertise in that area. This is the most efficient way for the project to proceed because everyone understands their role and is capable of completing their portion.

Based on the above, it is rather obvious delegation is useful in organizations. However, sometimes people delegate when they should be handling the work themselves….as is shown in the next section.

Reasons not to delegate

Delegation is also capable of being abused or misused as follows:

Laziness

Every employee has work-related aspects of their job that they do not particularly enjoy doing, but this does not mean they should pass that work on to others. If supervisors have important tasks that they need to attend to and their plate is full, then they should delegate menial work to their subordinates. However, if they delegate work simply because they do not want to do it, then that is a clear sign of laziness.

Organizational example

> Rhonda is a supervisor of the bakery of a grocery store. Part of her job is to check employee time cards to verify hours worked and note errors or problems. To do this, she needs to go to the time clock that is located at the front of the store. This means she has to leave her desk and walk several hundred feet…and that is something that she would prefer not to do.
>
> Rather than walk over to the time clock, Rhonda sends one of her employees to collect the time cards and bring them back to her so she can check them at her desk. After she is done, she has the worker bring the cards back to the time clock.
>
> The delegation of this task by Rhonda is wrong. She does not want to move from her desk to get the time cards, so she takes an employee away from his job to do it. A few minutes later, he has to leave his job again to take the cards back to the time clock. In this case, Rhonda's delegation is due to sheer laziness.

Power

Power can go to some people's heads to the point where they abuse it. In terms of delegation, this means that they believe their power gives them the right to delegate everything to others. While this might actually be true in some cases, it is not right…and it counteracts many of the benefits of delegation.

Organizational example

Jeffery is an office manager at an insurance company. He believes that he should never have to do any work because he has people to do it….he only needs to manage those people.

Jeffery delegates every task in the office, regardless of the size or importance. He does not even make coffee in the morning. Instead, he has a list that assigns the task to other office personnel.

Jeffery's insistence on delegating every task annoys and frustrates his employees. In fact, some of them avoid telling him problems because they do not want to be assigned the task of taking care of them. In this respect, the office does not operate effectively and many issues are not resolved.

Jeffries's power has gone to his head. He delegates everything, and this demoralizes his employees. In this case, power is abused and the delegation is counterproductive.

Qualifications

Work should never be delegated to employees who do not have the expertise to handle it. Some people ignore this rule, and the end result is problems for employees and organizations.

Organizational example

>Dr. Karen Hennie is a dentist who specializes in family care. She employs a dental hygienist named Jane to clean patients' teeth and assist her during other procedures. Jane has worked for Dr. Hennie for over ten years, and she is good at her job.
>
>Dr. Hennie's office is getting busier because the customer base is expanding, and she is having difficulty keeping up with the workload. To make things easier, Dr. Hennie delegates the job of reading X-rays to Jane. If Jane sees a cavity, she is instructed to set up an appointment for the affected customer within the next two weeks.
>
>This situation is not good. Jane is not qualified to read X-rays, and Dr. Hennie should not have delegated this task to her because an erroneous reading could be made. A mistake by Jane could cause problems for the dental practice, and it could potentially lead to a lawsuit.

Responsibility

Work should not be delegated when it is the direct responsibility of someone. If this happens, the work might not be completed in the most efficient manner….and in some cases, the work might not be completed at all.

Organizational example

>Nathan owns a law firm that employs seven attorneys. He is currently working on a case where he is defending a client named Anthony accused of armed robbery.

Nathan has done a lot of research to defend Anthony, and he is well-prepared for the case. However, another client needs his services the week of the trial and that client's case is worth a lot more money than Anthony's case. Due to this conflict, Nathan delegates Anthony's case to Janine, another attorney who works at the law firm. Janine will represent Anthony during the trial while Nathan works with the other client.

Nathan should not have delegated Anthony's case. Although Janine is a competent attorney, she does not have the knowledge to properly defend the client. Nathan has a moral, ethical, and legal responsibility to represent and defend Anthony during the trial.

Now that you are aware of some of the reasons to delegate and not delegate, let's discuss some general rules for implementing this workplace phenomenon. The next section lists strategic guidelines for situations that warrant delegation.

Delegation strategy

If it is decided that delegation is a good idea, then an implementation plan should be in place. That plan should adhere to the following six basic guidelines:

Match expertise

It is important to select the right employee for the job. Employees are easily discouraged when they do not have the expertise to handle a task that has been delegated to them.

Common errors

People often fail to plan here. Any employee is capable of delegating, but choosing the person with the right skills for the task is much more difficult. In terms of matching expertise, "failing to plan, means planning to fail."

Explain reasoning

Make employees aware of the reason for the delegation. They want to know why there are performing the task and what their contribution means…rather than simply being told to do it.

Common errors

Delegators often fail to realize the importance of an explanation. Employees take ownership of tasks when they understand why they are performing them, and this increased the chance of success. Essentially, employees want answers to the following three questions when they are given an assignment:

- What do I need to do?
- Why am I doing it?
- How does it benefit the organization?

Employees who do not get answers to the above questions feel like mushrooms...they are left alone to grow in the dark!

Define responsibilities

Let employees know exactly what is expected of them. This prevents time, effort, and money from being wasted due to a lack of understanding.

Common errors

Delegators who fail to define responsibilities do much more damage to organizations than they realize. Valuable resources are used by employees when they are not sure of their responsibilities. This means time and money are wasted until they understand exactly what is expected of them.

Encourage participation

Involve employees in the process by asking for their opinions. This motivates them to take action and inspires them to do their best.

Common errors

Delegators often fail here. Those who do not encourage feedback lose out on valuable information that could be provided by the employee doing the work. That information could be used to make the completion of future tasks faster and more efficient.

Follow up

Check-in with employees after they have been delegated tasks. Keep the lines of communication open for questions and comments. Follow-up is about being proactive rather than reactive.

Common errors

Some delegators do not establish a dialog with the people during the work. Open communication is necessary for answering questions that arise. Without communication, employees can get off track and spend time and effort doing unnecessary work.

Provide feedback

Let employees know how they performed after the project is completed. After all, these employees invested their time and effort, and they deserve to hear about the outcome. Additionally, compliments and constructive criticism help build relationships and assure success with the next delegated task.

Common errors

Feedback is often not provided by delegators. This is a mistake because feedback is important for making improvements in the future. Education is much more proactive in this sense because instructors are required to give feedback to students so they are aware of the areas they need to improve. In business, feedback is not required...so many delegators do not provide it.

Now that you understand a basic strategy for implementing delegation, let's move on to a discussion on ways to improve it.

Improving delegation

Delegation can always be improved, and the following are some suggestions for doing so:

Avoid micromanaging

This might be the most important part of improving delegation because micromanaging negatively affects workplaces in many ways. The following are factors affected by micromanagement in organizations:

Productivity

Employees become less productive when they are micromanaged. This is because they spend less time doing actual work, and they spend more time waiting for their supervisors to approve every task they complete.

Motivation

Micromanaged employees lose motivation due to the restrictions placed on them by their supervisors. When employees are not motivated, they do not perform to the best of their abilities.

Empowerment

Empowered employees are more involved employees because they take ownership of their jobs. Micromanaged employees are not able to take ownership of their jobs. They are not empowered because their bosses dictate their actions and make decisions for them.

Potential

This is one of the most serious and often overlooked effects of micromanaging. Employees who are micromanaged are prevented from learning new skills due to the controls imposed on them. Consequently, they never reach their potential for growth in organizations.

Creativity

Many people think that creativity is limited to artists, musicians, designers, and similar job descriptions. However, this is not true because creativity comes in many shapes and sizes. For example, an accountant can be creative by coming up with a new way to track costs for a meat processing plant. All the accountant needs is the freedom to experiment with different ideas….and then creativity begins to flow.

Micromanagers restrict their employees' freedom and prevent them from being creative. When this happens, organizations lose the potential for novel thinking that could make processes and procedures better, less expensive, or more efficient.

Innovation

Similar to creativity, innovation also requires freedom. When employees are micromanaged, that freedom comes with a very short leash that prevents them from using original thinking to come up with new ideas. Once again, organizations lose opportunities to get better.

Another interesting note about micromanagement and innovation involves secrecy. Micromanaged employees are not likely to share original ideas with their bosses because they fear their bosses will take the credit for those ideas. This makes sense because micromanagers have to approve every decision made by a subordinate…so they decide if, how, and when that idea will be released to people in higher positions.

Workload

This factor pertains to the supervisors doing the micromanaging. These individuals create a lot more work for themselves when they oversee every detail of their employees' jobs. At some point, this workload will become unbearable and stress will result. That stress is not good for supervisors, employees, or the organization.

Excessive workload is a good reason why supervisors should do a serious self-analysis of their management style to determine if they are micromanagers. This analysis could prevent a lot of unnecessary grief and aggravation.

Delegate uniformly

Uniform delegation means delegating consistently within organizations so it is not too much, too little, or too sporadic. Essentially, it involves three factors:

Avoid over-delegating

Delegation should never be excessive because employees get upset over being bombarded with work. As noted earlier, laziness and power are reasons not to delegate…and they are also reasons that people over-delegate.

Avoid under-delegating

People who refuse to delegate or do not know how to do so are under-delegators. This results in delays and work not getting finished. In short, people need to understand that they need to delegate to become more effective in their jobs.

Avoid crisis-mode delegation

People who only delegate during a crisis are not effective delegators. Delegation needs to be consistent throughout the year to prevent employees from believing that they only receive delegated tasks during problem times. The crisis-mode-only delegation also shows a lack of planning on the part of the delegator.

Provide resources

People who are delegated work need the proper resources to get the job done. This means they need people, equipment, information, time…or whatever else is required to complete the task. Delegators are responsible for providing access to these resources or they cannot expect the job to be properly completed.

Identify goals

Goals need to be communicated to people who have work delegated to them. This helps them understand what they need to do and why they are doing it so they can focus on the most important aspects of the task. In short, identifying goals increases the chances of success.

Summary

Delegation is critical for workplace effectiveness and efficiency. Without it, organizations fail to accomplish tasks and reach designated goals and objectives.

The eBook examines delegation in organizations. It discusses reasons to delegate, reasons not to delegate, delegation strategies, and ways for improving delegation. It is written for easy reader understanding using work-related examples for illustration and support.

Congratulations! You now understand more about workplace delegation…an important aspect of organizational behavior.

Brainstorming In Organizations
A Basic Understanding

Introduction — 77
Before — 78
- Homogenous team (non-diverse) — 78
- Heterogeneous team (diverse) — 78
- Idea transfer method — 79
- Reverse process method — 79
- Anonymous input method — 79

During — 80
- Establish rules — 80
- Establish objectives — 81
- Encourage participation — 81
- Encourage quantity over quality — 82

After — 82
- Other sessions — 82
- Apply results — 83
- Hiatus — 83
- Review, prioritize, combine, and refine — 83

Future — 84
- Age Diversity — 85
- Gender Diversity — 85
- Racial/Ethnic Diversity — 85

Summary — 86

Introduction

Organizations need ideas to grow and prosper, but developing, implementing, and maintaining those ideas can be a very challenging process. That challenge, however, can be minimized when employees work together in groups using a technique known as brainstorming.

Alex Osborne, an advertising executive, established the term "brainstorming" in the late 1930s in response to the customers his company lost during the Great Depression. It worked well, and he wrote about the phenomenon in his published books. Osborne alluded to brainstorming as a valuable problem-solving technique that has widespread application. It can be used for the resolution of problems ranging from simple to complex in many different types of organizations and industries.

Organizational brainstorming is essentially a group effort put forth by employees to find a solution to a problem. Similar to other groups in organizations, all members play an important role. They need to contribute using their personal strengths or the group as a whole will not function at peak efficiency. However, unlike other organizational groups, brainstorming groups do not have a leader. They often have a facilitator, but that individual functions more as a guide than a leader. His or her role is to keep things flowing and on track...not to make decisions or influence other members' thoughts or ideas.

Brainstorming groups also differ from other groups because, at least in the beginning, nobody's suggestions are discarded. In short, every brainstorming team member has equal status and there is no right or wrong. Does this seem too good to be true? It might, but it is the reality of the brainstorming technique… and it has been successful in organizations all over the world.

The premise of brainstorming is that every group member has different strengths that they can bring to the table for discussion. The exchange of ideas leads to solutions that individuals working alone are not capable of generating. This is not saying that a single person is not smart enough to come up with different solutions; it is merely saying that those solutions will be slanted toward that person's skills or expertise. For example, a sales manager does not have the same work experience as a production manager. They both understand how a manufacturing plant operates, but their jobs are completely different. The production manager views solutions to problems from a manufacturing perspective, while the sales manager views solutions to the same problems from a customer perspective. Who is right? The answer is both because there is no right or wrong in terms of brainstorming. All potential solutions are put on the table and the most effective are selected for cultivation and implementation.

A major advantage of brainstorming over other problem-solving techniques is the fact that it forces everyone in the group to think critically. Group members must entertain solutions from multiple perspectives, and this requires some deep thought. Sometimes it requires the problem to be broken down into smaller chunks for easier digestion. Other times it requires a broad analysis that meets the most important needs of everyone in the organization. Regardless of the way brainstorming is conducted, it is great for producing unbiased solutions to problems that affect employees in a wide variety of job functions.

A disadvantage of brainstorming is that some of the suggested solutions might appear to have little or no value to specific group members. If those members do not have the capacity to "think outside the box," then they might attack ideas that do not make sense to them; thereby creating a hostile situation.

If that situation gets out of hand, then dysfunctional communication can result where people are attacked instead of problems.

Ultimately, the good outweighs the bad for brainstorming, and that is why so many organizations utilize this technique for problem-solving. Let's move forward by examining the brainstorming process, starting with the activity that takes place before it occurs.

Before

Preparation is needed for brainstorming to be most effective, and that preparation starts with a diverse group selection. Diversity refers to traditional aspects such as race and gender, but brainstorming is more focused on position within the organization. Groups that are highly homogeneous (non-diverse) are at risk for groupthink which defeats the purpose of considering multiple ideas. Psychologist Irving Janus established the term "groupthink" to describe the process in which members make irrational decisions because they want to conform to what they believe to be the group consensus. In brainstorming situations, "irrational" means they do use their particular strengths for idea development. They follow the lead of others to avoid appearing dissenting or confrontational. They want to be known as a team player instead of a person who "goes against the grain." Since highly homogeneous groups tend to think alike, ideas from other perspectives are never given a chance. Heterogeneous (diverse) groups tend to think independently and are usually a better selection for brainstorming in organizations.

Please consider the following regarding group diversity:

Homogenous group (non-diverse)

These groups typically work well for problems that are short-term and require immediate action, such as an ambulance team making emergency calls to people who are in urgent need of medical care. Conflict is typically low in homogenous groups, but conflict is not a concern in brainstorming because all ideas are to be considered legitimate. Additionally, homogenous groups only represent a small portion of employees in the organization, and this is not good for brainstorming. For example, a homogenous group would be all office workers at a warehouse. These employees likely have good ideas, but their suggestions are not necessarily the same as the employees who perform the labor in the warehouse. A mix of both is needed for a good brainstorming session.

Heterogeneous group (diverse)

These groups accurately represent all employees in the organization. For example, a marketing manager, store manager, accounting manager, purchasing manager, customer service manager, quality manager, office manager, and human resources manager would be a good overall representation of people for a retail store chain. Heterogeneous groups are exposed to the thoughts of their coworkers, and this helps "outside the box" thinking for every member. These types of relationships often result in some conflict, but conflict is sometimes necessary for true brainstorming sessions. In most sessions, conflictive and innovative thinking is necessary to resolve problems...especially if those problems are long-term and complex.

Once the type of brainstorming group has been established, it is important to determine the number of members. This is not a simple task because every organization is different, but a general rule of thumb is no less than three and no more than twelve. Bigger organizations have more members in their groups because they have more people that need to be represented. However, the size of the organization alone does not always determine the number of people in a brainstorming group. For example, a large software company does not necessarily need the shipping manager involved in a brainstorming session about ideas for online advertising. The shipping manager might be of some value, but his presence is not necessary.

Once the group has been established and is ready for action, a brainstorming methodology (procedure) needs to be determined. There are several different methods for conducting brainstorming sessions, and it is imperative that one method is chosen and adhered to it to avoid confusion and wasted time.

Three common brainstorming methods include:

Idea transfer method

This method involves writing down a thought and passing it on to another team member until all members have documented their ideas. The thinking is that members will piggyback off each other's ideas or come up with new concepts that, in the end, result in a comprehensive list that can be narrowed down later. This method is advantageous because it forces members to think deeply to add to the list because they cannot write down the same idea. However, a disadvantage is that members feel pressure to "top" one another, and brainstorming should never be about competition or who is right.

An interesting note about the idea transfer method is that many employees are familiar with this technique they have experienced it at some time in their lives. They might have used the method in school to write a story or have fun with friends by laughing at what has been documented. In those instances, they were not necessarily trying to solve problems, but the basic concept of the idea transfer method was used.

Reverse process method

This method might appear to defeat the purpose of brainstorming, but it does work if followed through in its entirety. Instead of suggesting solutions, it involves coming up with more problems or ideas about what should not be done. That list is then used as a way to get members thinking in the opposite direction. Once they know what they cannot do, it simplifies the process of thinking about what they can do. For example, if the problem is to find a name for a new type of kitchen mixer, then the brainstorming session comes up with names that cannot be used. If members decide that "whirl" and "twirl" are not acceptable names, then any derivatives of those words are ruled out. This allows members to think freely without clouding their minds with unacceptable names.

Anonymous input method

Although brainstorming is designed to prevent groupthink tendencies, they can occur...and that is why anonymity is sometimes the best choice for brainstorming. This method allows employees to submit their ideas without other team members knowing they did so. Typically, this involves everyone writing their thoughts on paper and putting all of these pieces of paper in a common pile. Each idea is then read aloud, and group members accept or reject them. This method is advantageous because it prevents members from being embarrassed or humiliated if their ideas are rejected. It also removes personal ties or associations with ideas; thereby preventing a biased selection process.

The last important consideration before a brainstorming session begins is to set the date, time, and location. Avoid verbal commitments since these are easily forgotten and can cause a "he said, she said" war of words. An email is an acceptable way to do this, but it must be specific. For example, a non-specific email states "we will meet in the Houghton building in the early afternoon, sometime during the week of the 20th." This leaves room for a lot of misinterpretation, and it is non-committal. Instead, the email should state "we will meet in the Houghton building conference room at 1:00 pm on January 21st." Clarity is critical because lack of it can cause tardiness or attendance issues, and a brainstorming session that is delayed or canceled due to tardiness or attendance issues achieves little or nothing.

Now that you understand what needs to take place before brainstorming sessions, let's move on to the next section that tells what needs to take place during these meetings.

During

This is where the idea generation takes place. It is likely the most challenging aspect of brainstorming, but it is very rewarding if done properly. That being said, the following are important for properly conducting brainstorming sessions:

Establish rules

Once the group has assembled, it is important to establish ground rules. Below are three major rules that must be followed.

Stay on topic – Nothing has the potential to destroy brainstorming more than straying off the topic because it means the topic does not get addressed. Many brainstorming sessions have yielded little or nothing of value due to this problem, so it has to be an established rule. For example, a brainstorming session on the naming of a new product can easily get off-target by questioning whether the sales department is going to be able to sell it once it is made. Manufacturing is not the goal of the session and focusing on it severely hinders the chance of coming up with a good name.

No hierarchy – It must be made clear that nobody in the group is in charge of the decision-making. If one or more people control the idea contribution process, then the whole concept of brainstorming is undermined. For example, most brainstorming would probably be better off without the CEO present because he or she will likely influence every other employee's thinking. This is understandable because most employees want to please the top person in charge. After all, the big boss can likely do more for their careers than anyone else...but career advancement is not the reason brainstorming sessions are conducted.

No criticism – This rule must be clearly relayed to every member of the group because it is easily ignored or forgotten. Members who have been criticized or fear criticism will not put their ideas on the table because they do not want to be humiliated or embarrassed. A zero-tolerance for criticism needs to be implemented and any deviance from it must be immediately addressed. For example, a team member from production should not joke about the design suggestion of a team member from marketing. The production employee knows that the marketing employee could create design headaches due to a lack of manufacturing knowledge, but this type of criticism, regardless of the humor intended, does not belong in a brainstorming session because it will stifle creativity and open thinking.

Establish objectives

Brainstorming sessions are held for a reason, and that reason needs to be clearly established to assure every member understands what is expected of them. Objectives revolve around idea generation, but they can be made more specific to avoid misunderstanding and wasted time. For example, a brainstorming session designed to come up with an album name for a country band should clearly establish that this album is all covers of other artists' work. Based on this knowledge, members can rule out using "original recordings" or "brand new songs" in the album title because those phrases would be misleading.

Obviously, objectives will vary depending on the reason for the brainstorming, but they need to be established for organizational and productivity purposes. Without objectives, there is no direction and direction is necessary for goal accomplishment. People who have worked in organizations that lack objectives understand how frustrating it can be to try to do their jobs. In short, a brainstorming session without objectives is like a ship with no sail…incapable of going anywhere and destined to drift endlessly.

Encourage participation

Participation is important for just about every aspect of business, but that level of importance is taken up a notch for a brainstorming session. In fact, brainstorming is not possible without participation because letting one or two people take charge defeats the entire purpose of the session. Members should be reminded during the meeting that their input is critical for successful outcomes. This might seem like a relatively simple task, but it can be rather difficult due to the following reasons:

- Some members violate the rules. They stray off-topic, establish authoritative structures, and freely criticize others. Based on the *established rules* section in this book, it is understandable why some members refuse to participate.
- Some members are natural leaders and it is innate for them to take charge. They cannot resist the temptation to organize things and move forward, and they are very comfortable directing their fellow group members to follow their lead. These individuals are good at finding solutions to problems, but those solutions are typically biased and they do not take into account everyone's thoughts. In other words, those solutions defeat the purpose of brainstorming.

- Some members have a need to be a "big shot," so they speak out regardless of whether or not their words add value to brainstorming. These individuals often act more like cancer rather than the cure, and their major concern is self-promotion rather than problem-solving. They typically discourage participation from others, preferring to hear themselves over anyone else, and end up creating more problems that need to be resolved down the line. Obviously, this type of behavior is not good for brainstorming.
- Some members do not realize the importance of their input. They undervalue their ideas and see them as meaningless in terms of the big picture, so they refrain from adding to the discussion. Interestingly, this is the most common reason why participation lacks in brainstorming sessions, and it is likely the easiest area to improve with a little encouragement.

Encourage quantity over quality

In today's business climate, it is rarely good to emphasize quantity over quality. In fact, companies who promote a "quantity over quality" risk going out of business. Consumers want to know that quality is top-notch so they are assured that the products and services they purchase will meet their demands.

Brainstorming sessions are a rare exception to the "quality over quantity" rule. Employees engaged in brainstorming are encouraged to throw every idea on the table regardless of how impractical or ridiculous it might appear. Quality comes more into focus in future meetings as the suggestions are narrowed down to those that are best for resolving the problem.

Please keep in mind that quality is imperative for brainstorming sessions. Without it, solutions to problems would not be optimal; thereby defeating the purpose of the overall process. However, quality is not the main factor at the beginning of the sessions…and this should not change.

Now you are aware of important factors that need to be considered during a brainstorming session for it to be successful. However, there is still work to be done, and that is why the next section focuses on what happens after the sessions are completed.

After

The overall process of brainstorming is not necessarily finished after the sessions have been completed. In fact, there are a few directions that organizations can take as they address the designated problems. The following describes each of these directions for easy understanding:

Other sessions

Many times a single brainstorming session is not enough to resolve the problem. The results are a good start, but they must be further discussed in future sessions. Usually, the ideas that have already been generated are narrowed down to those that have the most potential for success, but members sometimes have the option of adding new thoughts. However, keep in mind that caution must be exercised or the group could find themselves starting all over again…which essentially defeats the purpose of the initial brainstorming meeting. Regardless of the risk involved, some companies have faith in multiple sessions and utilize them for a wide variety of brainstorming projects.

Interestingly, some brainstorming sessions are conducted with the absolute intent of generating future meetings. In these situations, organizational leaders do not believe the best results will be obtained from a single session, so additional group interaction is mandatory. Larger organizations are the most likely to follow this protocol because they have the time, money, and other resources to do so. However, smaller companies also adhere to the multi-session methodology if they believe the end results are worth it.

Apply results

Organizations that are happy with the results of a brainstorming session can begin the application process. This means the findings from the group interaction are put into action to make improvements or create new products and services. Application makes sense if everyone feels that the best solution to the problem has been found.

The importance of application should not be underestimated because it has a two-fold effect. As noted above, it puts ideas into action...which should always be the goal of any brainstorming process. However, it also motivates the group members who invested their time and effort in the project. They see concrete results of their hard work, and this encourages them to perform at higher levels on other job tasks. If nothing is done with their ideas, then they are much less likely to work hard on future projects because they do not see any type of reward system in place. Employees are not like horses who are continually motivated to move forward toward a "dangling carrot" that is never within reach. They need that carrot as a reward for their efforts, or they will not be motivated to work toward other goals required for organizational growth and prosperity.

Hiatus

Sometimes there is no direction taken after a brainstorming session. This is done for a few different reasons...some good and some not so good. It is good if members want some time to themselves to refresh, rethink their ideas, or deal with other aspects of their jobs. They cannot be expected to focus all of their time on a solution to one problem because they have other responsibilities. Anyone who has worked for extended periods of time on one project understands that a break is often justified and needed.

Unfortunately, there is a potential risk involved with breaks from brainstorming sessions. If the hiatus is too long, members can experience difficulty getting into the same frame of mind or remembering where the session left off. Similar to the problem mentioned in the *other sessions* section, this could lead to starting all over again. Worse yet, dysfunctional conflict can result from group members not having the same memory of what transpired during the brainstorming session.

Review, prioritize, combine, and refine

This is likely the most common direction taken after a brainstorming session. It is a fairly cut-and-dry process where all potential solutions are reviewed, prioritized, combined, and refined. This process is defined and exemplified below.

- First, the review process takes place which involves examining all of the ideas available for solving the problem. This encapsulates the entire process so decisions can be made to move forward. For example, the design of a new employee cafeteria includes ideas involving traditional based, cultural based, or modern based design.

- Next, prioritizing needs to take place by ranking ideas in order of importance. This is where the elimination process takes place by removing the solutions that make the least sense. For the cafeteria, it is determined that a traditional based design makes the least sense because it is the least motivating to the predominantly younger workforce.

- Then, the remaining priorities need to be examined for possible combinations that might make them work better. In the cafeteria, a combination of cultural and modern based design is considered a potential solution even though it might not transpire.

- Finally, the remaining ideas are refined into the best possible solution and that solution is put into action. It is decided that a modern design is best for the cafeteria, so that will be the way the organization proceeds.

Now you know what happens before, during, and after a brainstorming session. Since so many organizations use this process, it must have some value. However, will that value be enough for organizations to continue using brainstorming in the future? This question is answered in the next section.

Future

Without a doubt, brainstorming will be a valuable tool for improvement and idea generation in the future. However, it will change due to the impact of technology and diversity. In terms of technology, sessions will not always require members' physical presence. Geographical concerns will no longer present themselves as people are able to log into discussions from all over the world. Technology also offers speed that was inconceivable a short time ago. Ideas can be exchanged with others via a few clicks and searching for specifics within those ideas can be done by typing in as little as one word. This means large volumes of data can be received and perused by employees in just a few seconds….and this process is continually getting faster. Transactions that used to take days can now be conducted in a few minutes, and this helps when time is a major factor in problem resolution.

Diversity will also shape brainstorming sessions. In organizations, diversity is a topic of increasing importance as different kinds of people enter the workforce and organizations move into the global marketplace. Gone are the days when married White Anglo-Saxon Protestant (WASP) men ran businesses while women and minorities were steered away from higher positions in the workplace.

Also gone is the thinking that disabilities and sexual preferences need to be hidden, older people are of little value despite their knowledge, and only people with money are important. While the working world is far from perfect, it has come a long way in the past half-century....and it has impacted the ideas generated from brainstorming.

The following shows how different types of diversity will impact brainstorming in the future:

Age Diversity

Age diversity is unique because every person in the organization falls into this category. Employees might not look the same, act the same, think the same, possess the same amount of money or education, or belong to the same race, culture, or religion...but they all fall somewhere on the age spectrum. The number of years separating their age creates the diversity factor.

Many organizations use multiple generations of people for brainstorming sessions because these people grew up in different time periods and did not encounter the same life experiences. That being said, they do not always share similar viewpoints and will have different ideas.

Gender Diversity

Traditionally, the term gender has referred to men and women. However, this has recently changed to add a third category known as transgender. For the sake of simplicity, this section will only focus on males and females.

In organizations, gender diversity refers to the representation of male and female employees in the workplace. Up until the 1960s, jobs were classified and designated as being for men or women. The positions available to women were limited, and higher-level management jobs were designated for men only. Times have changed since then, and the government is now involved in preventing gender bias in organizations.

Male and female employees work together to accomplish tasks and achieve organizational goals, but they have different perceptions about the jobs they perform. This is good for organizations during brainstorming sessions. Different ideas lead to better problem solving and prevent gender-specific thinking. Quite simply, men and women have different job skills, product knowledge, and personal experience that inspire their creativity and help them generate ideas.

Racial/Ethnic Diversity

This type of diversity is based on people and their linkages. These people include Asians, Blacks, Latinos (Hispanics), Native Americans, and Whites who are associated with their skin color, ancestry, culture, or nationality.

In organizations, racial/ethnic diversity refers to the representation of the groups mentioned above in the workplace. Similar to gender diversity, many of the best jobs in the past were only available to white people, and minorities were forced to take lower-paying positions. Once again, the government stepped in and now monitors workplaces to prevent racial/ethnic bias in organizations.

Today, people of all different colors and backgrounds work together every day in many organizations across the United States. They strive to accomplish the same objectives, but their ethnic and racial differences play a role in their perception of the workplace and the way they are treated by management. These variances lead to debates on best business practices, and they change the ideas generated in brainstorming sessions.

The future of brainstorming in organizations is best summed up by saying that it will play a powerful role in problem-solving. Group members' differences will work to make the process better because a wider variety of employee thoughts are shared during the idea generation process. Brainstorming is here to stay, and it will become more important as organizations seek to become more stable and market-relevant.

Summary

Brainstorming is the process of using group thinking for idea creation. It adds value to problem-solving because group members have different backgrounds and experiences that lead to solutions that cannot be generated by individuals thinking alone. It has worked in the past, it works now, and it will continue to work in the future as employees search for new ways to help their organizations grow and prosper.

This book examines brainstorming in organizations. It analyzes the process before, during, and after its implementation while discussing its value for idea generation and problem-solving. Brainstorming has been around since businesses were created, and it not going away any time soon.

Congratulations! You now understand more about brainstorming in organizations...a valuable process for idea generation.

Hands-on Leadership
A Basic Introduction

Introduction	89
Advantages	89
Vision	89
Decision-making	90
Motivation	91
Application	91
Disadvantages	92
Micromanagement	92
Friendship	93
Non-realistic	93
Motivation	94
Key traits	94
Stability	94
Knowledge	96
Authenticity	97
Confidence	97
Future	98
Authoritarian	98
Paternalistic	99
Summary	100

Introduction

It is a known fact that leaders make and break organizations. Similar to conductors of orchestras, they guide and motivate employees to perform to the best of their ability. However, unlike orchestra conductors, they are not always front and center in full view of their workforces. Some leaders are invisible because they push from behind while others are off on the sidelines focusing on matters they deem more important.

Front and center management styles are usually more successful than back or sideline styles because employees are like a piece of string. Leaders in the front pull that string and move it forward, leaders in the back push it into a crumpled-up mess, and leaders off to the side do nothing with it at all. Without the ability to move forward, organizations do not progress and their survival is threatened.

Hands-on leaders always occupy front and center positions in their workforces. They are in the trenches with their ears to the ground listening for indicators of change. They demonstrate by example, blending their abilities and skills into their work to show employees how things should be done. They are not afraid to do the same work as their employees and often work side-by-side with those employees to reach organizational goals and objectives. In short, hands-on leaders inspire others with their actions and carefully avoid the dreaded "do as I say, not as I do" management mentality.

This book examines hands-on leaders. It discusses their style, highlights their advantages, exposes their disadvantages, identifies their key traits, and discusses their role in the future. The text is educational and informational, and it is written for easy reader understanding at all levels.

Let's move on to the first major section of these books that discusses the advantages of hands-on leadership.

Advantages

Most people who have worked for leaders who are hands-on realize those leaders have a huge impact on their workforces. They influence the way employees work, solve problems, collaborate, and make decisions. Their efforts are relentless with the goal of doing whatever is best for their organizations. This helps companies move forward and, when done correctly, can grow small businesses into large businesses.

A simple search of the internet will show many different organizations that started with hands-on leadership. In fact, this is the way most small businesses begin...sometimes because they choose to do so and other times because they have no choice due to the limited resources that are available. However, regardless of the reason for the use of hands-on leadership, it provides some big advantages that are listed below.

Vision

Vision is necessary to establish the direction organizations will move in the future. It encompasses organizational culture, values, beliefs, and purpose to see what needs to be done for growth and prosperity.

Based on the above, truly visionary leaders do the following:

Define the future using realities of the present and experiences from the past

Hands-on leaders fit this definition well because they understand where they need to be in the future, deal with the present on a daily basis, and have a wealth of applicable past experience. These assets are explained in more detail as follows:

They understand where they need to be in the future – Hands-on leaders have their finger on the pulse of their operations. They know where their organizations need to be, and they know they are the best people to guide their employees in pursuit of that destination.

They deal with the present on a daily basis – As the name says, hands-on leaders are "hands-on" when working. They know what is happening in their organizations because they are always actively involved. No other style of leadership is better for understanding what is going on with everyday operations, and this is critical for visualizing the future of organizations.

They have a wealth of applicable past experience – The real estate saying "location, location, location" means successful selling is determined by the location of the lot or structure being offered. This is true, and it has application in organizations. However, the saying changes to "experience, experience, experience" because experience often determines the success of companies. Hands-on leaders place themselves in the "heat of the battle" which results in them acquiring a wealth of applicable experience for determining where their businesses need to be in the future.

Every organization needs a leadership vision to grow and prosper. Hands-on leaders are often visionaries because they are able to assess challenging situations and formulate improvement plans. They work well with employees who help them put their plans into action and achieve organizational success.

Decision-making

Good decision-making is critical in organizations for many different reasons. It is important for attracting customers, keeping employees content, increasing productivity, facilitating processes and procedures, reducing the impact of regulations, and improving financial health. In short, it has a huge impact on the bottom line and is the biggest reason why businesses succeed or fail.

Unfortunately, many organizational decisions need to be made when problems are mounting. Difficult circumstances require decision-making under less than ideal conditions, and hands-on leaders work well with this type of adversity. Their ability to handle pressure stems from the great understanding they have for their organizations. They are rarely in the dark on something because they are involved on a daily basis, and this gives them the ability to analyze situations and make good decisions…even if those decision decisions require immediate action.

Hands-on leaders are often the best choice for leading organizations that are in challenging or difficult situations. They are comfortable in their workplaces and find balance in stressful environments. Combine this with the harmony they have with their employees, and it is not a surprise their decision-making is rarely hasty, unreasonable, or poorly constructed.

Motivation

Many theories have been developed for workplace motivation. A fairly well-known example is the Goal Setting Theory created by psychologist Edwin Locke. This theory is based on the thinking that employees should set specific and somewhat difficult goals that lead to higher work performance. It challenges the idea that workers should simply "do their best" because that type of thinking does not motivate people to perform at peak levels.

Another workplace theory regarding motivation is the Equity Theory developed by psychologist J. Stacy Adams. Adam's based this theory on the thinking that employees compare their work to that of others and make decisions based on that comparison. Fair and equitable treatment in the form of recognition and/or rewards motivates them to perform their jobs to the best of their abilities.

Both of the theories mentioned above have been used in organizations to help inspire workers. However, hands-on leadership is often the best way to motivate employees to perform optimally because those employees see their leader working alongside them. The motivation provided by hands-on leaders is genuine, and nothing about it is theoretical. Their passion for accomplishing the goals and objectives of their organizations shines through as they inspire others to reach peak levels of job performance.

Hands-on leaders also motivate others by providing examples of what needs to be done and how it should be accomplished. They perform their jobs to the best of their abilities, stay focused on tasks, avoid shortcuts, show up to work on time, and maintain a positive attitude while doing so. This positive behavior inspires employees to act the same...especially if those employees see successful results from their efforts.

One last important aspect of motivation involves listening. Hands-on leaders inspire others in the workplace simply by listening to them. Their close working relationships with their employees allow them to hear and comprehend the problems those workers are experiencing. Employees appreciate the fact their concerns are being heard by a person who has the authority to make changes...and this appreciation inspires them to keep progressing.

Application

Every type of leadership style has important elements that make it the best choice for management. For example, authoritarian leaders want their organizations to be as efficient as possible, and they believe order and structure are the keys to achieving that efficiency. Direct supervision is important and subordinates are kept on a leash for control purposes. This works well for leaders of government agencies that require tight control. An example is a US border patrol supervisor. He makes sure his subordinates follow rules precisely, and he does not let allow them to make decisions without his approval.

Transformational leaders also have significant elements that make them a good choice for management style. They work tirelessly to get personnel to think independently about what is best for organizations. They believe the keys to success involve setting objectives that drive employees to work harder and increase performance. In short, the goal of this leadership style is to "transform" employees' thinking so they want to work toward improving their organizations and taking them to the next level.

Mutual fund managers with large portfolios often use transformational leadership styles. They set goals for their employees who purchase stocks for the funds, and they make sure the goals are worthwhile so the employees work hard to achieve them.

Hands-on leadership is unique because, except for laissez-faire, it can be incorporated into every type of leadership style. A leader can be authoritarian, democratic, paternalistic, transactional, or transformational and still use a hands-on approach. This means hands-on leadership can be applied to a wide variety of organizations and industries; thereby making it the most versatile way to manage.

Now that you have been exposed to some major advantages of hands-on leadership, it is only fair to discuss the negatives of this management style...so let's move on to the next section.

Disadvantages

Not surprisingly, there are also some negatives associated with hands-on leadership. The following explores some of the disadvantages that have the potential to occur when managers lead from the front and center of their organizations:

Micromanagement

The most obvious disadvantage of a hands-on management style is that it can lead to micromanaging. In fact, there is a fine line between hands-on leadership and micromanagement...similar to that between a genius and a crazy person. Leaders who cross that line can go from productive and inspirational to destructive and demotivating.

Micromanaging leaders are typically strong decision-makers because they understand the needs of their organizations. However, they often have difficulty delegating and become upset when their subordinates make a decision without their approval. Many times subordinates are perfectly capable of making decisions, but they are not allowed to do so by micromanaging bosses. This delays tasks from getting completed, hinders organizational efficiency, and prevents goals and objectives from being accomplished.

Micromanaging leaders are also self-absorbed. Their narcissism leads to them believing that their ideas, thoughts, and decisions are the best...so they should be in control of every aspect of job tasks. This controlling presence has the potential to upset employees, regardless of their talent, attitude, or disposition.

One of the biggest problems of micromanaging leaders is the fact that they typically do not admit to falling into this category. They often fail to realize they are controlling, narcissistic, overbearing, and domineering. They deny micromanaging and instead claim that they are organized and conscientious, and they are only doing what is best for their organizations. Since they are not aware of their actions, they have no plans for changing their behavior.

In short, micromanaging leaders hinder productivity by monitoring processes and procedures far too closely. They are similar to bullies due to the high level of control that they maintain and their refusal or inability to delegate or relinquish that control. Based on this, it is rather obvious that the potential for hands-on leaders to turn into micromanagers is a concern that can destroy organizations.

Friendship

In some respects, this disadvantage is the opposite of micromanaging. Friendship might seem more like an advantage than a disadvantage, but that is not the case for some organizational leaders who use a hands-on management style. The problem occurs when employees working alongside leaders become too friendly and take advantage of the situation by becoming less productive. They are not motivated to perform at peak levels because they are "chummy" with the people in charge. This can cause the demise of businesses when they are no longer able to compete due to higher labor costs.

In short, hands-on leaders who treat their workers as buddies rather than subordinates can severely hinder their organizations. This problem intensifies when these leaders show favoritism toward certain workers with whom they have established the closest relationships. Employees who are not favored become resentful, and this causes them to lower their own productivity or search for employment elsewhere. In a relatively short period of time, friendship from hands-on leadership can snowball into a major issue for organizations and employees.

Non-realistic

Hands-on leaders are not always honest about their organization. This is not saying that they lie; it is merely saying that they do not always view things realistically because their involvement in their businesses makes them overly passionate about their visions of growth and prosperity. Their passion is good because it inspires others to work toward the same goals, but it also causes them to ignore reality in some situations. For example, a hands-on owner of a candle factory believes so strongly in a new type of longer-lasting wick that she keeps investing money and time into that wick even though it has proven not to work.

If employees detect non-realist leadership attributes, they can lose faith and trust in those leaders' abilities and objectives. Their motivation to work hard is reduced significantly, and the organization suffers. Workers respect hands-on leaders who take risks and venture into the unknown, but they want to see light at the end of the tunnel or that respect is lost.

Another issue with non-realism is the lack of ability to see the organization as a whole. Hands-on leaders are often unable to view the entire picture because they are caught up in day-to-day activities. For example, they can become so consumed with production levels that they lose sight of quality. When this happens, the company suffers and the only way to resolve the situation is for the leaders to remove themselves from daily production activities...which means they need to become less hands-on.

Motivation

How can motivation be a disadvantage when it has already been listed as an advantage? The answer is that high-achieving employees do not need motivation to improve their job performance. When hands-on leaders try to inspire these individuals, they find it annoying and unnecessary. In fact, motivation attempts by their bosses actually hinder their performance and do more damage than good. In short, the motivation attempts made by a hands-on leader end up backfiring.

The worst part about the backfiring of motivational actions is that it can lead to more severe problems that cannot be corrected. If hands-on leaders do not back off, then they risk losing high-performing workers to organizations with bosses who are not always trying to inspire improvement. The room for improvement is limited for high-achievers, and hands-on bosses need to realize this when working with them.

Now you understand some of the disadvantages that can result from hands-on leadership. These negatives can be quite destructive, but they can be overcome if hands-on leaders have the ability to properly implement and maintain this management style. This leads us to the next section that identifies key traits of hands-on leaders.

Key traits

There is no standard definition for leaders. They come in a wide variety of shapes and sizes and use different management styles for their workforces, so they cannot be grouped into one category. However, as noted in the advantages section, many of them use a hands-on approach to guiding their employees. That being said, there needs to be an understanding of the key traits of hands-on leadership that lead to success. The following are some of these key traits:

Stability

Stability is a rather broad term, so exactly what does it refer to in terms of hands-on leadership? In short, it refers to balancing workplaces so everyone works together to achieve goals and objectives. This is done by motivating employees to do their jobs to the best of their abilities using controlled rewards or praise. "Controlled" is important because not enough rewards or praise demoralizes employees and excessive amounts cause them to become complacent or demanding.

Rewards are usually money based that come in the form of raises, bonuses, profit-sharing, or 401K contributions. If money is tight, then paid time off is an option. If money is an issue and paid time off cannot be granted, then stock options can be offered. Wise hands-on leaders understand they can get creative when motivating employees via financial rewards.

Praise is given verbally, in written form, or through some type of social media. Employees can be told they are doing well through face-to-face interpersonal communication. They can also be praised in written form via a company-wide email, or their good work can be tweeted so people inside and outside the organization know about it. Wise hands-on leaders understand there are multiple ways to motivate employees with praise, and they also know that "a pat on the back" goes a long way.

Emotional stability is an important aspect of stability that warrants discussion in this section. Hands-on leaders must be able to remain composed during challenging situations because their behavior is very visible to the employees that surround them. They also need to understand the needs of their employees and listen to their problems for moral boosting reasons. They must develop relationships with employees that establish bonds of trust…but the boundaries of those relationships need to be monitored to avoid employees from taking advantage of the situation for their own personal gain rather than that of their organizations.

Good hands-on leaders understand the value of trust as it relates to stability. They know that lack of trust affects many different factors within their organizations including:

Fairness - If employees do not believe they are being treated fairly, then they lose trust in the hands-on leaders who are treating them unfairly. This is critical because workers are dependent on their organization to earn a living. They spend a good portion of their waking life at their place of employment, and they need to believe they are being treated fairly to build trust.

Honesty - This is likely the most important factor for building trust. Lack of honesty from leadership prevents trust from building in almost every instance. Employees need honesty from hands-on leaders to help them identify with their organizations. This identity makes them feel an active part of the culture, and it motivates them to help their organizations achieve goals and objectives.

Dishonest leadership lowers employee morale and productivity. In terms of management-employee relations, honesty is almost always the best policy. Without hands-on leadership honesty, there is no employee trust.

Respect - In terms of building trust, respect is in a category by itself. It is not always perceived as important, but anyone who has attempted to build trust without respect knows that this perception is far from reality. Employees will be more productive if they are respected. They want leaders to listen to them because they have acquired a wealth of knowledge that can be very useful for the management of people and processes. If hands-on leaders do not listen, then employees lose trust that those leaders are doing what is best for their organizations.

Communication - This is the most obvious factor involved in building trust. Communication is necessary for sending messages that carry meaning, and that meaning is used to build trust. Employees lose trust when hands-on leaders do not communicate with them. They want truthful information about their organizations so they know what is happening within them. Without communication, employees are lost without a guide.

Collaboration - Collaboration is the most overlooked factor in building trust. It is important because people who work together build relationships, and trust grows from those relationships. Employees need to work with each other to form relationships that lead to trust-building. Without collaboration, people do not learn to trust each other...and this is something that hands-on leaders need to take into account.

Stability comes naturally to many hands-on leaders, but those that do not innately have this trait can improve in this area. Over time, they learn what to do and what not to do to get their employees to work towards objectives and goals. They find a balance between being a boss and being a friend, and they act accordingly to do what is best for their employees and their organizations. This is not easy, but it is important to separate the good hands-on managers from the not so good.

Knowledge

This refers to (1) knowledge of the jobs being performed and (2) knowledge of human nature. Knowledge of the jobs being performed is the most obvious aspect of this trait because leaders who do not understand the jobs of their workers are not hands-on. They cannot help others complete job-related tasks because they do not know how to do those tasks. In fact, leaders who are not hands-on actually hinder day-to-day operations when they get involved. Employees are put through a painful process because they know more than the person who is supposed to be leading them. This process is demoralizing and, worse yet, it lowers productivity.

Knowledge of human nature is also important for hands-on leaders because their words and actions motivate their employees to perform at peak levels. Hands-on leaders must know how people are going to react in specific situations to prevent problems from occurring. This ability comes partially from the experience of being in similar situations, but it also stems from a basic understanding of employee behavior. Unfortunately, many leaders lack this understanding...and that is why they are not capable of succeeding with a hands-on management approach.

Knowledge of human nature also involves understanding employees' emotions because workers can be encountering non-job-related problems that affect their job performance. They simply cannot perform at peak levels due to the negative feelings that dominate their thoughts. In these situations, hands-on leaders must be able to show empathy and compassion to help employees get back on track.

Empathy might appear to be counterproductive because hands-on leaders are sympathizing with the employees; thereby enabling them to decrease their productivity. However, it must be remembered that this is a process that eventually yields positive results. Employees who are normally good at what they do are worth the time and effort spent to get them back to high-performance levels. Wise hands-on leaders realize that the investment of time and effort is sometimes necessary or they risk losing those employees completely.

In short, hands-on leaders must be able to show their employees the best ways to get jobs done, but they also must have an understanding of those employees' needs and feelings while employing that methodology.

Authenticity

Hands-on leaders need to be authentic because those who are not come off as being full of useless rhetoric...more commonly known as being full of "bullsh*t." Employees can tell when leaders are pretending to perform jobs that they are not capable of doing or acting as if they understand something that they clearly do not.

Authenticity also helps hands-on leaders to earn the respect of their employees. They do what they say they are going to do, and this leads to respect that cannot be achieved by leaders who are not hands-on. Their behavior inspires employees to do their best, even when times are difficult. In short, authenticity is directly related to productivity...and productivity often drives the bottom line.

The last reason authenticity is an important trait involves modeling. When hands-on leaders conduct themselves in realistic ways, they model the traits that they want to see in their employees. Those employees are then motivated to overcome the challenges necessary for success. The old saying "actions speak louder than words" has application here because, in terms of motivation, authenticity is the action.

Confidence

Confidence is important for any leader, but it has extreme significance for hands-on leaders because they are working alongside their employees. They must exhibit strength and understanding of the situation to get their employees to buy into their vision. If their confidence begins to diminish, so will their employee's efforts...and some workers might begin to look for new places of employment.

Every organization is challenged in some way, and confidence is necessary for hands-on leaders to face those challenges. Decisions need to be made that keep organizations headed in the right direction and prevent situations from getting out of hand. "Wishy-washy" leaders are unsure of organizational direction, and this often leads to them making wrong decisions or, worse yet, no decisions at all.

Confidence also involves curiosity. Yes, believe it or not, curiosity is a key trait of hands-on leaders. They need to be inherently compelled to always look for new ideas and better ways....regardless of whether it involves going against the grain or challenging the status quo. This means hands-on leaders need to be committed to learning. They have to be aggressively watching for people or things that can give their organizations an edge in markets that are becoming increasingly competitive.

It must be noted that there is a difference between confident leaders and cocky leaders. Confident leaders use their knowledge and experience to make calculated decisions. They are gambling with their future, but that gambling is based on past successes in similar situations. Cocky leaders lack the knowledge and experience to make sound decisions. They "shoot from the hip," and this results in them taking uncalculated risks that have a greater chance of failure than success. In short, confident leaders are conscious and logical while cocky leaders are usually the opposite.

As indicated above, there are several important traits needed for hands-on leaders. These traits lead to success, and that success means hands-on leadership is very useful. However, this raises a question that needs to be answered. Is there a point when hands-on leadership has outlived its usefulness? This question requires thought because hands-on leadership is the best management style available for leaders who want to better understand their workforces. Based on this statement, every leader should utilize some form of hands-on practice…but hands-on practices are not always best for organizations. Like it or not, there is a point when hands-on leadership should be abandoned in favor of a different style. Usually, this time comes when an organization becomes too big for anyone to stay actively involved by working alongside employees on a daily basis.

Future

This section might be the most important discussion in this book because hands-on leadership will never go away. This is a fact, not a prediction, because some leaders have no choice other than to be hands-on. However, this management style will need to change to meet the demands of business. Hands-on leaders will need to become more creative as their organizations compete for market share. They will need to do more with less as resources dwindle and demands increase.

The internet has made it relatively easy to get into the global marketplace without a large number of employees or large amounts of time and money spent. Companies such as Amazon.com allow businesses to ship products all over the world. For example, music and books can be sold digitally in every corner of the globe. More impressive is the fact that music and books can also be sold in a physical format because they can be manufactured on demand and distributed worldwide. This means that more and more small businesses have the opportunity to market globally…and hands-on leaders need to react accordingly.

The following shows how hands-on leaders will need to change for two specific types of management styles:

Authoritarian

As noted earlier, authoritarian leaders want their organizations to be as efficient as possible, and they believe order and structure are the best way to achieve efficiency. Control is essential for these individuals, and they maintain close supervision so they do not lose it. They see other types of leadership style (such as democratic) as inefficient because control is limited. Platoon leaders in the military often experience success using authoritarian leadership when leading their troops in battle.

In business, authoritarian leadership is helpful for organizations where employees are not working together toward a clear and common goal. It unifies workers and provides direction by creating order through structure and discipline. Many businesses have been brought back from near bankruptcy to profitability by authoritarian leaders due to the management techniques implemented.

Like it or not, hands-on leaders who employ an authoritarian leadership style are going to need to change. These individuals are great for providing a vision that prevents organizations from wandering, but that vision often comes at the expense of their employees' freedom...which is something that most employees dislike. This dislike will cause authoritarian leadership to decrease as a whole, which will force hands-on authoritarian leaders to change their management techniques.

In short, employees need freedom and creativity at work to find job satisfaction. That feeling exists today, and it will not change in the future; thereby forcing authoritarian leaders to alter their styles.

Paternalistic

Paternalistic leaders are exactly what the word implies...they act as a parent to their employees. They are more like a mother or father figure than a supervisor because they take charge of their workers' lives inside and outside of work. They show concern by supporting employee ideas, protecting their best interests, encouraging them to give their best effort, and providing rewards for their success. In return, they expect loyalty from their employees...just like parents expect from children.

Hands-on leaders use the paternalistic style of management because it builds self-confidence. Employees work hard due to their loyalty to the organization, and this pays off in terms of goal accomplishment. A feeling of success develops as they move on to their next task, and they build the self-confidence necessary to accomplish other goals. Essentially, a positive cycle results where employees build confidence, attain goals, and help their organizations achieve objectives.

It is likely that this type of leadership style will become less prevalent in the future. Work-life balance will increase in importance, and that means employees will increasingly want to separate their work lives from their personal lives. Some organizations will find paternalistic leadership beneficial, but the style will diminish as a whole...and hands-on leaders will need to adjust.

The style of management will also diminish because hands-on paternalistic leaders value employee relationships that are personal and professional...and this is simply not possible in businesses that grow in size. Leaders will not be able to interact one-on-one with all of their employees, so change will be required to properly manage their operations.

The last reason that hands-on paternalistic leaders need to change involves technology. Paternalistic leadership will have no value for organizations that promote telecommuting because the personal element is missing. Hands-on leaders will need to realize this shortfall and adjust accordingly.

In short, hands-on leadership will continue to play an important role for organizations all over the world, but that role will need to change to keep up with organizational growth, employee needs, and technology. Leaders who refuse to adjust their styles need to remember the following:

Change is painful, but resistance to change is futile.

Regarding the above statement, hands-on leaders who choose not to "roll with the times" are risking the future existence of their organizations.

Summary

Hands-on leadership is one of the most common types of leadership in the world. It has been around for many years, and it will be here for many more to come...simply because it is successful. It is used by a wide variety of leaders with different styles; thereby making it very versatile in application.

Hands-on leaders are always in front of their workforces, often performing many of the same job functions as their employees. They are very visible, work well with others, demonstrate by example, and exhibit confidence that is contagious. In terms of success, they are outdone by no other types of leaders.

This book examines hands-on leadership by discussing its style, advantages, disadvantages, key traits, and future. The text is educational and informational, and it is written for easy reader understanding at all levels.

Congratulations! You now understand more about hands-on leadership...a management style that paves the way for organizations all over the world.

Psychopathic Employees in Organizations
Bad For Everyone

Introduction — 103
Traits — 104
- Deceitful — 104
- Egotistical — 104
- Insincere — 104
- Shallow — 105
- Remorseless — 105
- Threatening — 105
- Charming — 106

Types — 106
Specific professions — 109
- Police officer — 109
- Doctor — 109
- Lawyer — 109
- Professor — 109
- Media personality — 110
- Preacher — 110
- Government official — 110

Consequences — 110
Detection — 112
Preventing — 113
- Confront — 114
- Avoid — 114
- Run — 114

Summary — 114

Introduction

The terms psychopath and sociopath are often used interchangeably, and this is understandable because they have many similarities. Both are considered to have mental issues, both tend to mirror the image of their targets to gain those targets' trust, and both are dangerous because they destroy relationships with others. However, these two types of individuals also differ because sociopaths can learn their behavior while psychopaths are born with their state of mind. Another difference is the fact that sociopaths often withdraw from society for certain periods of time, while psychopaths are typically relentless when trying to achieve their goals. Psychopaths might give up on their current targets, but they immediately move on to others until they find a victim. In this respect, psychopaths are fearless with no conception of right and wrong...which is not always the case for sociopaths.

This book focuses on psychopaths in the workplace. These deranged employees are intent on destroying the careers of their coworkers by doing whatever they believe is necessary. They tend to follow a pattern or protocol where they win over the confidence of others and then attack them when they are not expecting it.

Workplace psychopaths have no problem being deviant or cruel...often enjoying this type of behavior while executing their plan. They rarely fear being caught and enjoy the thrill or challenge involved. One of the most disturbing things about workplace psychopaths is the fact that they are never remorseful for their actions, so they practice the same behavior over and over with the only difference being their victims.

Although psychopaths represent a small portion of most workforces, they present a serious concern due to the problems that they cause. For example, a high-ranking executive who is psychopathic sets the tone for the entire organization. His actions cause others in lower positions to exercise the same behavior causing the company to suffer as a whole. Ethical standards are lowered and corporate responsibility is kicked to the curb. In short, the culture of the company changes due to the psychopathic leader.

Interestingly, the percentage of psychopathic employees in organizations exceeds that of psychopaths in the general population. Some estimates rank psychopaths as three to four times more likely to be found in workplaces than in the public. Add this to the fact that many of the corporate "crazies" are in leadership positions, and it is relatively easy to understand the pain and suffering they are capable of inflicting on others.

Psychopathic employees that are not in leadership positions are often charming, funny, and sincere...and they attract people to themselves with relative ease. They con their coworkers into doing work for them that they should be handling on their own. Their coworkers "blindly" do what they are asked to do, and this strokes the psychopaths' egos and encourages them to do more of the same. Adding insult to injury, psychopathic workers take credit for work that was done by the employees who they conned.

Now that you have a basic concept of workplace psychopaths, let's move on to the next section that discusses specific traits of these individuals.

Traits

Workplace psychopaths are only concerned with themselves. They have their own agenda and will do whatever is necessary to accomplish that agenda. In this regard, psychopathic workers are unique, purposely separating themselves from the rest of the workforce. However, the fact that they are all classified into the same group (psychopathic employees) indicates they have certain traits in common.

Every psychopathic worker is a little different, so it would be virtually impossible to list all of their traits. However, some of the more general traits are listed below along with a description of each:

> *Deceitful* - This is a nice way of saying something that is not nice...the fact that psychopathic employees are pathological liars. They will say anything to anyone to get what they want with no regard for the negative impact that it may cause their coworkers or their organizations. There is an old saying that goes "Oh what a web we weave when we practice to deceive." Psychopathic employees are notorious "web-weavers" with the lies they create. Unfortunately, other workers get caught in those webs and find it difficult to break themselves free.
>
> Psychopathic employees also deceive coworkers by refusing to take responsibility for misjudgments, errors, or mistakes. They immediately blame others even though they know they are guilty, and they stick to this story regardless of the facts that are present. This embarrasses, stresses out, and/or infuriates coworkers who are wrongly accused...and they are sometimes never able to prove their innocence.
>
> The last area of deceit that deserves mention is related to plagiarism. It involves stealing other employees' work or taking credit for work that is not theirs. In some instances, employees plagiarize the work of others without actually knowing that they are doing something wrong. For example, they might use part of a coworker's research without knowing how to properly cite or credit that coworker. In these cases, plagiarism is unintentional and the offenders simply need to be properly educated. However, unintentional plagiarism is not the case when psychopathic employees are the culprits. They know exactly what they are doing and are only interested in themselves. They understand that there is a risk of getting caught, but they thrive on that risk and will lie if accused of any wrongdoing.
>
> *Egotistical* – Confidence is something that is good for employees to have in many instances. It helps them make decisions and proceed in the ways that are best for their employers. However, overconfident employees can create problems. They are opinionated and always believe they are doing the right thing....regardless of what is happening around them.
>
> Psychopathic employees take confidence to a new level. Their confidence is so high that they are excessively conceited and self-absorbed. They have little regard for the thoughts or feelings of others and believe they rightfully deserve to be the center of attention for everything because they are superior. They are also narcissistic and not afraid to brag about their work or personal accomplishments. In other words, they are egotistical.

Insincere – This is an often overlooked trait of psychopathic employees because so many other issues associated with them are at the forefront. They are insincere in terms of what they really intend to accomplish. They come up with new ideas, but expect others to follow those ideas through in the workplace. They have no intention of doing the work necessary to put their thoughts into action, even though they make it appear as if they plan to do so….which means their coworkers are left toeing the line.

Coworkers who are successful in implementing the ideas of psychopathic employees are in for an unpleasant surprise because those psychopaths take full credit for that success. However, as might be expected, psychopathic individuals are the first to place blame on others when things do not work out as hoped or anticipated. In terms of sincerity, psychopathic workers are malicious based on their cruel and wicked behavior.

Shallow – This refers to emotions that are on the surface only. Psychopathic employees are able to put on a different "mask" for every coworker. That mask changes frequently because it is solely based on the objectives of each person. This is not only deceiving, it is also unethical because there is no regard for right or wrong….from a legal, business, or moral standpoint.

Psychopathic employees prefer to meet one-on-one with coworkers rather than in groups because they do not want witnesses who can uncover their masks. Based on this, it is not surprising that they find ways to avoid meetings. They are well aware that they are deceptive individuals, and they prefer to remain on the sly rather than get caught.

Remorseless – With all the problems that psychopathic employees cause, one might think that they would be sorry for what they have done. Remorse, however, is not part of the psychopath's makeup. They do not feel the pain of others and have no problem making false promises or conning others to reach their goals.

Some people consider remorseless to be the absolute worst trait of psychopathic employees. They understand that people do wrong to others, but once that wrong is exposed there should be some type of remorse for the actions taken and the resulting problems. Unfortunately, psychopathic workers lack this emotion, and that is why they are able to continually behave in ways that negatively impact people and organizations.

Threatening - Psychopathic employees have nerves of steel, so they can change their personalities at a moment's notice. They are performers who can act quite well and appear threatening when doing so. They alter their voice tone or volume by making derogatory comments, injecting sarcasm, or yelling loudly. These types of actions make up what is known as verbal aggressiveness, and it intimidates coworkers and makes them uncomfortable.

Psychopathic employees also display threatening non-verbal cues that indicate seriousness if other employees do not comply with their requests or demands. They raise fists, throw hands up in the air, point fingers, shake heads, frown, grit their teeth, and position their bodies so they invade the space of others. This behavior is not spontaneous as some people are led to believe. Non-verbal actions of psychopathic workers are planned in advance and utilized when necessary, clearly showing the deviant nature of these destructive individuals.

Charming – This is likely the most devious trait of psychopathic employees, and that is why it is saved for last. Many of these predators tend to be friendly, funny, agreeable, and personable…all of which are aspects of charm. They give off a vibe of being approachable, and they appear warm toward others. This personification naturally attracts coworkers because those coworkers want to be accepted and liked.

Charm is good…so why is it bad for psychopathic employees? The answer is because it is a facade. The charm is used to suck in others, and then stab them in the back when the opportunity arises. Psychopathic workers are sly and calculating, and they know that they can get what they want by winning over others. After they achieve a likable status, they make the moves that reveal their true colors.

Now that you understand some major traits of psychopathic employees, let's move to a discussion of the types of these workers that exist in workplaces.

Types

The word "deviance" has a negative image associated with it for many people. This is because it refers to actions outside of established rules and regulations. Some deviance is worse than others, but it all violates some type of predetermined norms.

Deviance in organizations is known as workplace deviance. Workplace deviance is the purposeful act of harming employers and employees. These actions violate workplace standards, regulations, rules, and norms with the intent of doing mental or physical damage to people or organizations.

Psychopathic employees are extreme workplace deviants, and they behave in ways that cause problems for people and organizations. That being said, these individuals need to be better understood so they can be minimized or eliminated in workplaces. This starts by understanding the specific types of psychopathics listed in this section.

The first type of psychopathic employee is known as the con artist. These individuals give new meaning to the word "shyster." They are unscrupulous and fraudulent, but their deceptive behavior is geared toward coworkers who work for the same company and are on the same team. They have no problem attacking those who work with them if it helps them get what they want…and guilt or remorse never enters their minds.

Con artists often use manipulation as a strategy. They operate under false pretenses and establish trust based on the target employees' belief that good things will transpire. Their victims start out feeling motivated, but they end up feeling manipulated after trust in the relationship is violated. This loss of trust often starts when con artists break deals or fail to hold up their end of bargains. They make guarantees or promises with no intention of following through. When confronted about their lack of action, they make up lies to defend their position or blame the problem on someone else. Nothing is ever their fault, and they make sure other employees are well aware of their innocence.

An interesting note about psychopathic con artists is that some of them get so caught up in their own lies that they lose track of the truth. They cannot distinguish between reality and the things they have made up, so they cannot be honest even if they truly wanted to make an effort. It is much easier for these individuals to live in a fantasy world at the expense of others than it is for them to accomplish goals and objectives with truth and honesty.

The second type of psychopathic worker is known as the justice giant. These employees take action on coworkers they view as immoral or unethical because they want justice to prevail. Their goal is to "right the wrong" done by someone else. However, there are many different opinions about what is immoral or unethical, so these individuals are only achieving justice for themselves without regard for others…including their victims.

An example of a justice giant is an animal lover employee who vehemently disagrees with any form of hunting. She makes up lies about one of her coworkers who is an avid deer hunter to try to get him fired. She says she has seen him bring pornography into the workplace, and he has sexually harassed her. These lies damage the reputation of the hunter and could damage his career if they are believed by others.

Justice giants will lie, cheat, deceive, and scheme to achieve their objectives. They are rigid, rarely deterring from their actions, because they believe they are doing what is truly right. They lack emotional stability, and because of this have no remorse. Based on their behavior, justice giants become the same as the people they seek to destroy because their actions are viewed as immoral and unethical by their coworkers.

Predators are the third type of psychopathic employee. As indicated by the name, predators prey on their workplace victims, even to the point of stalking them, to further the agenda. They seek out specific employees that they believe will help them accomplish their goals without regard for the impact that their negative actions have on those employees.

Unfortunately, some psychopathic workers prey on others for sexual gratification. For example, predatory psychopathic male employees stalk their female victims with the intent of dominating them sexually. Think about a minister in a religious organization who seeks out a young and attractive female member. He knows he has some control over this woman, and he uses that power to coerce her into sex with him. Essentially, this sex is without the consent of the female, but the power of the minister makes it appear as if it is the right thing for her to do.

Something worthy of mention regarding predatory psychopathic employees is the fact that they are likely to get hostile if things do not go their way. They verbally attack their victims and bad-mouth them to others in the organization. This behavior has the potential to make the victim submit to the psychopaths' demands rather than face the repercussions of degradation and humiliation. This never ends well emotionally or psychologically for victims, and they almost always get hurt.

The fourth type of psychopathic employee is known as the captivator. Captivators know how to win people over and "sweep them off their feet" with compliments and kind words. They are verbally gifted and always know the right things to say to others. They appear to care about their victims and use emotionally comforting phrases to draw them closer. The employees being targeted feel relaxed and at peace because they believe they have met a person who understands and admires them…only to be attacked, left out on a limb, or backstabbed later on.

Some psychopathic workers are captivators because they believe something is owed to them. They believe other employees have received more than them in terms of accolades or rewards, and they want to even the score. Driven by a desire for retribution, they pretend to form friendships with their victims; thereby developing a bond. In time, they use that bond to victimize their "friend" and further their own agenda. They believe their actions are justified, and they are likely to repeat the process by targeting others unless they are prevented from doing so.

In short, captivators are nasty employees with no concern at all for others. These individuals are despicable because they are so insincere and deceiving. Their goal is to climb the social ladder to promote themselves, and they have no conscience about the coworkers that they crush in the process. Unfortunately, most employees do not unmask the captivator until after they have been scammed and the damage has been done.

The fifth type of workplace psychopath is known as the power freak. These individuals are intent on controlling everything, and they are unyielding in their efforts. They are probably the most aggressive type of psychopathic worker due to their insistence on having it all. They tenaciously cling to the belief that their self-worth is much higher than that of other employees, and this gives them the right to be in charge. Power freaks are capable of handling themselves in any type of verbal fight and have even been known to resort to physical altercations to get what they want.

Some power freaks garner attention by becoming "bad boys" in organizations. They bend or break rules and have no fear of doing so. This lack of fear sometimes leads to them getting in trouble with those in higher positions, regulatory agencies, or court systems. They are not always successful, but their behavior attracts others because they look like mavericks or pioneers paving the way to something better. Unfortunately, the only ground-breaking that power freaks do is to that beneath the feet of their victims.

In terms of psychopathic employee behavior, power freaks are typically the "best of the worst" for organizations and the employees being targeted. They are often the shortest-lived type of psychopathic employees due to their greed. They fall from grace because they want too much, too fast. Once they are discovered, the negative perception of them snowballs and ultimately leads to their demise. In other words, longevity issues make power freaks the easiest type of psychopathic employees to eradicate from workplaces.

The sixth and last type of psychopathic employee is the occupier. These individuals are in positions of power, and they use those positions to take advantage of others with their only interest being themselves. Their actions impact many employees and, as a result, their victims can be quite large in number.

Many times occupiers are highly educated in professional fields, such as lawyers or doctors, and they are well aware that their position enables them to control others. Their psychopathic behavior goes beyond ruining their victims' jobs or careers. For example, doctors and dentists hurt the careers of others in their practice, but they can also endanger the health of their patients due to their reckless actions.

Occupiers are unique psychopathic workers because they can move on when they are discovered and things start to work against them. Their credentials allow them to seek out and accept similar positions in different organizations, where they resume their psychopathic behavior and negatively impact a new group of employees. This means occupiers have the potential to spread like a disease without a cure. They are cancer, and they must be stopped before they destroy their hosts.

Now that you understand some major types of psychopathic employees, we can move on to the next section that identifies specific professions that these individuals occupy.

Specific professions

After reading everything in this book so far, it is quite obvious that workplace psychopaths care only about themselves, calculate their menacing moves with precision, and have sinister plans in place for accomplishing their objectives. They avoid guesswork as they target specific employees and prey on the vulnerabilities of those individuals. After being discovered for whom they really are, some of these diabolical workers disappear with little or no notice...only to surface again somewhere else and do the same thing. In short, psychopathic employees manipulate others for furthering their agenda unless they are caught.

Not surprisingly, employees with high levels of psychopathic behavior are often in positions of power. That power can come from overseeing others or by simply possessing authority due to position or knowledge. Higher positions are reached due to experience or specialized education. For example, a plant manager might have been a laborer and a supervisor before reaching his current position. Along the same lines, a CPA in the same company might have been hired due to her accounting degree.

The following are examples of positions occupied by workplace psychopaths:

> *Police officer* - These civil servants are in a great position to exploit their authority with very little chance of resistance. Their word is often final, and they are well aware of the power they possess. Psychopathic male cops have been known to coerce unwilling females to perform sexual favors due to the fear of repercussions for not doing so. They have no conscience and do not care about the feeling of their victim because their only objective is to please themselves.
>
> *Doctor* - Doctors are assumed by most people to be very knowledgeable in the medical profession. After all, they spent a lot of money and time going to medical schools where only the brightest students are admitted. Unfortunately, some doctors are psychopaths who only care about themselves. They look to satisfy their own egos and they accomplish this by controlling their patients with their opinions or "advice." Many patients have no idea that they are being taken advantage of because they firmly believe their psychopathic doctors are only doing what is best for their health.
>
> *Lawyer* - Psychopathic people are often attracted to the legal profession with the goal of becoming practicing attorneys. This is because they know their clients will believe they have a wealth of knowledge, and those people will do whatever is asked of them to win their case or get out of a troubling situation. Psychopathic lawyers are "snakes" that will exploit their clients for their own benefit...stopping at almost nothing to get what they want.

Professor - College professors are very capable of swaying the minds of their students, especially those who are young with limited experience working in real-world organizations. Students believe their professors are worldly and knowledgeable, and they absorb the rhetoric of those professors like a sponge….regardless of whether it is true, valid, or reliable. These "brainwashed" students are held mentally captive by their professors, and this puts them in the dangerous position of being easily manipulated for the sole purpose of furthering their professors' agendas.

Media personality – This refers to radio, television, internet, and print people who have established followings. Their words and actions sway their audiences to think and behave in certain ways because those audiences believe in them. Media personalities become psychopaths when they go on "power trips" that cause their followers to take action that helps nobody other than themselves…and this can end up causing a wealth of damage to people and communities.

Preacher – Any form of a priest, rabbi, minister, reverend, or counselor falls into this profession. Similar to media personalities, preachers have a lot of power over their followers, and this power can cause many problems. Unfortunately, psychopathic preachers have the ability to coerce people into doing drastic things, even killing themselves or others, for the sole reason of achieving their personal goals. If this is the case, then everyone loses….and the damage cannot be undone.

Government official - This refers to government employees who have some type of regulatory power over organizations under their jurisdiction. Financial auditors and safety inspectors are examples of employees who can use psychopathic behavior to coerce others into doing things that are not required, unethical, or just plain wrong. Bribes can become expectations, favorites can be played, and discrimination can become the norm…all due to the actions of psychopathic workers.

Politicians are government officials that warrant special attention in this category. They face scrutiny from a variety of different individuals and organizations, so the ability to persuade others is essential for their survival and re-election. However, this persuasion can turn into manipulation…and that is when politicians become psychopathic employees of the government.

Now you understand the traits and types of workplace psychopaths along with some common professions that they tend to occupy. Armed with this knowledge, it is time to move on to a discussion on the actual harm that these perpetrators do….also known as consequences.

Consequences

After reading what has been written so far in this book, it should not be surprising that many consequences result from psychopathic behavior in workplaces. For example, bullying is quite common because employees who are taken advantage of by psychopathic coworkers often feel as if they are coerced. They are pushed into thinking or acting a certain way, they feel pressure to conform, and they feel there will be consequences if they choose to act differently. Workplace psychopaths push hard to accomplish the agenda they have set forth for themselves, and they have a "take no prisoners" attitude.

This means they destroy everything and everyone that is an obstacle…and sometimes this is best done by assuming the role of bullies.

If employees can no longer tolerate the problems caused by a psychopathic coworker, then they can either fight back or they look elsewhere for employment. Those who choose to fight have a real battle on their hands because psychopaths are self-driven and are not easily dissuaded from their wrongdoing. Those who do not think the fight is worth the time and effort simply look for a different employer. These individuals do not want to get mad, and they do not want to get even…they just want to get out. For this reason, turnover is a consequence of psychopathic behavior in workplaces

Firings are a form of turnover, but they deserve special mention when caused by psychopathic employees because they are so wrong and unfair. Employees who are falsely accused of wrongdoings by psychopathic coworkers can be fired for their alleged actions. These firings are perplexing, disturbing, and infuriating to the people who are the victims, but the decisions to get rid of them have been made so they need to accept it and move on. If the psychopathic employees are exposed for what they really are, liars and con artists, then management realizes their error…but that realization is too late to repair the damage.

Some employees choose to remain with their organization in the face of attacks by psychopathic coworkers. These individuals might want or need to stay with their current employer, but they strongly dislike contact with the psychopaths… so they combat the problem by skipping work for a day or more. They intend on coming back to their jobs, but the time away from work allows them the peace of mind necessary to remain sane. This absenteeism might be good for the employees if they can afford the lost wages, but it is not good for their employers. Organizations need people to come to work, or those people would not be employed. When employees miss work, some of their job tasks simply do not get accomplished. It does not take a genius to figure out that a string of unaccomplished tasks can lead to efficiency and profitability issues.

Organizations with high turnover and absenteeism due to psychopathic actions still need to get work done, so they turn to the employees who are still employed and show up to work. These employees are valued because management knows they can be counted on to get the work done. They are "rewarded" for their effort and loyalty by taking on a heavier workload. As employee workloads get heavier, their job satisfaction diminishes. When job satisfaction decreases…productivity decline is sure to follow. Productivity is life-sustaining for most organizations because without it those organizations fail and cease to exist.

Psychopathic employees, especially those in leadership positions, can disrupt the entire workplace. If this happens, employees start to bicker among themselves about responsibility and accountability-related issues. The blame game starts and dysfunctional conflict is inevitable. Conflict can be good if it is functional, but dysfunctional conflict is always destructive. Dysfunctional conflict pits people against each other in verbally aggressive rather than argumentative confrontations. Principle goes out the window, people are attacked rather than problems, and the end result is warring factions in the workplace. Eventually, very little gets accomplished and the bottom line is negatively impacted…all due to psychopathic workplace actions.

Ethics are also negatively impacted by psychopathic workers. Organizational ethics are formal and informal guidelines that regulate all employee actions. They describe how people should behave in workplaces and combat employee activities that management deems unacceptable. In short, these guidelines establish ideas of right and wrong...and unethical actions set undesirable precedents. Psychopathic employees violate ethical guidelines, especially when they are in leadership positions, and their actions cause everyone else to take a step backward.

Corporate responsibility was mentioned earlier as being "kicked to the curb" by psychopathic employees. A major aspect of corporate responsibility is social responsibility. Essentially, social responsibility is an obligation to act in ways that benefit society. For organizations, this means the stakeholders (people with have an interest in the organization's success) must make sure that there is a balance between their economy and the environment. Psychopathic leaders destroy the social responsibility of organizations, and employees and society suffer.

Possibly the most important consequence of psychopathic behavior in the workplace is the loss of trust...which is why a discussion on trust is saved for last in this section. Trust is important because, as many people are aware, building it is a challenging endeavor. It takes time and effort to build the relationships necessary to establish trust, and that trust can be broken with a single action...something psychopaths do on a regular basis.

Trust building for organizations is no different than it is for people in their personal lives. Employees work with each other, customers, and suppliers to establish relationships...and those relationships build eventual trust. However, many factors play a role as those relationships are being built. For example, employees want to be treated fairly. If they do not believe they are being treated fairly, then they lose trust in those who are treating them unfairly. Psychopathic employees, especially those in higher positions, treat their coworkers unfairly...and trust is lost

A factor related to trust is honesty. Honesty is sometimes overlooked for its importance, but, in reality, it might be the most important factor because the lack of honesty prevents any type of trust-building. Psychopathic employees are notoriously dishonest, and this means they are never trusted after being discovered for their true selves.

Another factor related to trust-building is respect. Respect is not always perceived as important, but anyone who has attempted to build trust without respect knows that this perception is far from reality. Employees will not communicate or collaborate with coworkers who they do not respect. Collaboration is important because people who work together build relationships, and trust grows from those relationships. Employees lose respect for psychopathic workers, and trust becomes a major workplace issue.

Obviously, the consequences of psychopathic workplace behavior show that it needs to be prevented. Prevention starts with detection...the focal point of the next section.

Detection

Psychopathic employees should be fairly easy to identify in the workplace, but they often go unnoticed until it is too late. Coworkers need to be careful when they are around these individuals, but many times the opposite is true because they let down their guard when they are won over by the offenders...until the attacks begin. There is no upside to psychopathic behavior in organizations, and, as the sub-title of this book states, these types of workers truly are "bad for everyone."

This section identifies some of the warning signs displayed by psychopathic individuals. The first sign is psychopathic employees' uncanny ability to handle pressure. Psychopaths often have "nerves of steel" and are not easily rattled. They are comfortable with work-related tasks that stress out their coworkers, and they readily accept challenging assignments. The reason for this comfort is due to the fact that they have no intention of completing those assignments. They will pass the responsibility on to someone else via some type of scam or they will do nothing at all. Either way, they will not follow through with completing the job...so there is no reason for them to feel pressure.

Lack of follow-through leads to another indicator of workplace psychopaths known as insincerity. Quite simply, psychopathic employees are unreliable...even though they appear to be the exact opposite. They build trust with coworkers and then destroy that trust when by not doing what they say they are going to do. Insincerity is a big indicator that leaders in organizations should be aware of at all times. Unfortunately, many leaders drop their guard after becoming comfortable with workplace psychopaths, so this type of behavior goes undetected.

Leaders should also watch out for overly friendly psychopathic behavior. Employees who "try too hard" to befriend coworkers are potentially dangerous because they could be working on those people for the sole purpose of furthering their agendas. Over time, trust is violated and workers feel hurt because they were taken advantage of and betrayed.

Interestingly, another indicator is the exact opposite of friendly. Those who show no empathy or refuse to apologize for undesirable behavior could potentially be workplace psychopaths. This insensitivity might even be taken to a higher level...that of anger. Some psychopathic employees get mad easily, make threats, or ask aggressive questions that frustrate or embarrass their coworkers.

Aggressive employees can be very competitive, and competitiveness is a type of behavior that is also associated with workplace psychopaths. This is not saying that competition is bad, but workers with egos that drive them to compete for everything, regardless of the importance, could be trouble. Unfortunately, competitive employees often rise to the top of organizations, and their psychopathic tendencies are not discovered until their power is so great that nothing can be done.

The last indicator of a workplace psychopath is secrecy. As mentioned earlier in this book, workplace psychopaths are pathological liars. They do not want to get caught in their lies, so they do not want people listening to them as they speak. They avoid meetings and large gatherings because there are too many witnesses, and they often use the excuse that they are too busy to stop what they are doing. In short, employees who constantly pull their coworkers off to the side for private conversations should be watched closely to assure they are not doing this for the sole reason of accomplishing their personal goals.

Now you understand some indicators of psychopathic workers. The next section suggests strategies that can be used by employees to prevent themselves from being victimized by these individuals.

Preventing

Psychopaths will always exist in workplaces because there will always be deviant workers who want to further their own personal agendas. However, employees can take action to avoid becoming victims of these predators. Essentially, prevention involves three different strategies as follows:

Confront

This is the fight strategy, and it involves "calling out" psychopathic employees for their actions. This strategy can be quite successful due to the fact that many psychopaths give up after they are exposed. They do not want a fight on their hands, so they move on to try their manipulative behavior at other organizations. Their negative actions will not stop because they will go on elsewhere, but the employees who confronted them will be safe from experiencing their wrath.

The strategy of confrontation works, but it does not come without risks. If management does not view psychopathic employees as threats, they might side with these deviant individuals and promote them. When this happens, the psychopaths are sure to take revenge on those who confronted them before they reached their positions of power.

Avoid

One way to prevent being a victim of workplace psychopaths is to not play their game. Some employees simply do not get involved with these deviant individuals by avoiding them at all times. They do not make deals with them or form bonds with them, and they keep their guard up at all times. This strategy might seem a bit insensitive, but it prevents employees from being exposed to the damage that workplace psychopaths are capable of doing.

It must be noted that, similar to confrontation, the avoidance strategy is a calculated risk that can backfire. If psychopathic employees end up reaching high levels in organizations, they are sure to take down those who did not work with them to achieve their self-centered goals. Avoiders end up on psychopathic leaders' hit lists, and their careers typically end or come to a complete halt.

Run

This strategy is a last resort, but it is one that might need to be used when there are no other realistic choices. It mainly applies to workplaces where psychopathic employees take over the top leadership positions of organizations, such as the president or CEO. Psychopathic leaders can control the entire culture of organizations, and their actions become the norm. At this point, there is little choice other than to leave the infected organizations for other employment.

Unfortunately, this strategy is not uncommon. People simply cannot or do not want to deal with the aftermath of workplace psychopaths, so they move on to other companies. The saddest part about this is the fact that the psychopathic leaders could have been prevented from reaching top positions in their organizations if attention had been paid to their actions when they held lower-level jobs. Instead, their behavior was seen as benevolent rather than threatening, and they received promotions when they should have received reprimands.

Summary

Workplace psychopaths exist in every type of workplace. They often destroy employees and organizations, especially if they are in positions of power, and they have no remorse for doing so.

This book examines psychopathic employees. It explores their traits, describes their types, defines their professions, examines the consequences of their actions, discusses methods for their detection, and suggests prevention strategies for those affected by them. The text is informational and educational, and it is written for easy understanding at all reader levels.

Congratulations! You now understand more about psychopathic employees...an unfortunate, but realistic, occurrence in workplaces all over the world.

Drug Abuse in Organizations
Explaining, Understanding, and Preventing

Introduction — 118
- Safety — 118
- Healthcare — 119
- Absenteeism — 119
- Turnover — 120
- Profitability — 120

Drugs targeted — 121
- Heroin, codeine, morphine, and other opioids — 121
- Marijuana, hashish, and other cannabis — 121
- Liquor, beer, and other alcohol — 122
- Speed and other amphetamines — 122
- Cocaine and other stimulants — 122

Testing methods — 123
- Urine — 123
- Hair — 123
- Saliva — 124
- Breath — 124
- Blood — 124
- Sweat — 124

Prevention — 125
- Written — 125
- Oral — 125
- Electronic — 126
- Management — 126
- Non-management — 127

Summary — 128

Introduction

Illegal and legal drug users impact the financial well-being of the taxpayers in the United States. Sometimes, this impact is understandable, such as when diabetics receive insulin at no charge because they have no health insurance. These people are at risk of dying if they cannot get insulin, so it makes ethical and moral sense to supply them with the drug for free. Other times, however, the financial impact is not understandable or justifiable. An example is people using opiate-based drugs to get high rather than to combat pain. These individuals are also at risk of dying, but that risk is self-inflicted due to their drug abuse. After prolonged use, they will do whatever is necessary to get high...including committing crimes and causing others financial, emotional, and physical pain.

Unfortunately, the pain caused by people who abuse drugs often extends beyond their personal lives and affects the people they work with at their places of employment. Their detrimental actions can impact entire workplaces causing businesses to lose money or, in severe cases, go out of business. These consequences are possible because drug abuse does not have boundaries when it comes to who it affects. It can happen to any employee including owners, so it should not be surprising that some companies have shut down after drug abuse impacted their top leader or leaders.

The following are some shocking statistics on workplace problems resulting from drug abuse as reported by American Drug Testing Drug-Free Workplace Advisor (volume 1, issue 92):

- American businesses spend over 100 billion dollars per year on legal and illegal drug abuse.
- 15% of employees in manufacturing operations, including those in higher management positions, admit to illegal drug use.
- Over half of job-related accidents are caused by drug abuse.
- More than one-third of employee theft comes from employees who abuse drugs.
- Drug abusing employees miss work ten times more frequently than drug-free employees.
- Turnover of drug-abusing employees is 30 percent higher than drug-free employees.

Based on the above statistics, it is understandable that many organizational leaders require drug testing on their employees. This testing can be structured or random, but it is always designed to detect illegal drugs that employees have consumed for the following reasons:

Safety

This is considered the most important reason by many people because it involves the safety of the employee under the influence of drugs as well as his or her coworkers. Workers who are impaired on the job risk the physical well-being of themselves and others if they are not able to perform the basic tasks required for their positions. This is especially true when heavy equipment or machinery is operated because a lot of weight and force are involved.

When employees abuse drugs, they lose the ability to remain cautious while working. They are much more likely than clean coworkers to take shortcuts, override safeties, or fall asleep on the job. These deviations, regardless of their severity, put the safety of all employees at risk. Since safety is a top priority for many companies, it is understandable that those companies are requiring employees to submit to drug testing.

Healthcare

Health care is a benefit that has great significance for most employees because they want to make sure their families are covered for medical expenses when health issues arrive. Catastrophic problems, such as a heart attack or cancer, can cost hundreds of thousands of dollars. Without health care coverage, most people simply could not afford to pay these high bills. Based on the importance of health care, it is understandable that many people make career choices based on the benefits available to them.

Any business person who deals with employee health care understands that the cost of that healthcare continually increases. Due to this increase, healthcare is becoming a major reason for drug testing. Employees who require medical treatment for drug-related damage to their bodies or minds cost their employers a lot of money due to the care required to get healthy. These costs add insult to injury because damage to drug abusers is self-inflicted and could have been avoided.

Absenteeism

Most companies employ people because they need them to complete the work necessary for profitability. Managers expect their employees to show up for work every day that they are scheduled unless those employees are sick or experience unforeseeable circumstances. Drug abuse leads to people missing days at work, and the costs of this absenteeism can be catastrophic as shown by the following:

> *Decreased productivity* – When employees are not present to do their jobs, the amount of work that is normally completed begins to decrease. Productivity continues to go down until these employees show up for work and do the jobs that they were hired to do. In short, decreased productivity becomes a major issue when absenteeism rears its ugly head.
>
> *Increased workload* – Employees who miss work might or might not be aware of the added tasks that other employees need to take on in addition to the work involved in their own jobs. However, regardless of this awareness, absenteeism increases the workload of the people who show up for work. If that work becomes too excessive, then it does not get done...and the goals and objectives of organizations do not get accomplished.
>
> *Unnecessary turnover* - If absences are prolonged, the added work can turn into a serious problem as the workers who are charged with the additional responsibilities begin to look for other employment. These employees might have been content with their jobs at one time, but their minds change when they are forced to complete the tasks of those who fail to show up for work.

Unfair perception – Most people have experienced a time in their career when they simply did not feel like going to work. However, they know that others depend on them to complete tasks, so they go to work and do their jobs. Unfortunately, employees who abuse drugs typically do not have that same mindset. They do not care if others need them because they are only concerned with what is best for their own personal needs...which is often consuming more of the drug that they are abusing.

Hindered communication – Absenteeism disrupts organizations because it affects balance, and unbalanced workplaces create a disruptive environment that hinders communication between employees. Anyone who has worked in an organization with poor communication understands the negative consequences. Some of these consequences are minor, such as not understanding the details of a specific process, while others are major, such as not meeting a customer's deadline. However, regardless of the severity, hindered communication leads to problems.

Elevated stress – Stress is a concern in many workplaces because it leads to mental and physical health issues. If it is not controlled, it can lead to people leaving for other jobs, going off on disability, and, in extreme cases, taking legal action against the company that brought on their stress. Unfortunately, absenteeism increases stress because employees are forced to do the work of their absent coworkers. Drug abusers are notorious for missing work; thereby increasing the stress levels of their coworkers.

Turnover

Absenteeism can lead to people being let go from organizations, but it is not the only reason why employee/employer relationships are severed. Some employees choose to leave organizations of their own free will simply because they no longer have the desire to work...and drug abuse contributes substantially to that desire. In fact, drug abuse is sometimes the only reason people quit their jobs. Their only goal is to get high, and work interferes with accomplishing that goal.

Turnover is a major concern for companies due to the costs associated with it. People have to be hired and trained, and the time and money spent doing this can be lost if the new employees do not work out. Faced with the problem of a revolving door, companies are using proactive measures to maintain their current workforces, and drug testing is one of those measures. The goal is to detect the problem early and prevent it from snowballing into something that cannot be corrected in the future.

Profitability

Some people associate profit with greed. In certain situations, this association is accurate....especially when that profit is not shared with the people who helped bring it to fruition. However, profit is necessary for organizations to grow and prosper. Without profit, new employees will not be hired and existing employees will not get pay raises.

Regardless of the stigma associated with profitability, it is paramount for most companies...and it is adversely affected when safety, health care, and absenteeism are impacted by drug abusers who drain valuable resources by missing work and not performing at expected levels. Add to this the risk of theft by these individuals, and it is understandable how a financially sound company can turn into a company struggling to survive as employee drug use escalates.

Many of the above issues work in combination to create problems in organizations. However, regardless of the way these issues intertwine, it is understandable that companies make the reduction of absenteeism a major goal...and drug testing of employees plays a role in achieving that goal. This process might not seem fair to some people, but it does make sense in a world where a lot of senseless drug use takes place.

Now that you have a basic understanding of why organizations test employees for drugs, we can move forward to a discussion on the types of substances targeted by this testing. The next section examines the various types of drugs that organizations look to find in employees.

Drugs targeted

Leaders of organizations are concerned with any type of drug abuse, but some substances take precedence over others. Below are some common drugs that employees abuse.

Heroin, codeine, morphine, and other opioids and opiates

Opioids are quite likely the biggest drug concern facing society today. In fact, opioid abuse is so high that it has reached epidemic proportions and, unfortunately, this level is not expected to diminish anytime soon. This means society will suffer negative consequences….and so will organizations.

Opioid abuse garners a wealth of attention because it often stems from legal prescription drug usage. Prescription drugs can only be authorized by a licensed professional. This means a doctor could be supporting an addict's habit. However, regardless of whether the drugs were obtained legally or illegally, they are addictive and cause problems for workplaces.

Some opioids are so notorious for their negative effects that they have become household names. Legal painkillers such as Oxycodone, OxyContin, and Vicodin of these drugs are well recognized throughout the world. Heroin and morphine are also well-known names, but they are often illegal opiates.

Employees consume opiates and opioids for the euphoric feeling that these drugs are capable of producing. However, these drugs also result in drowsiness, irritability, and the inability to properly focus on jobs...so the abusers and their coworkers suffer. Additionally, workers who take synthetic opioids, such as fentanyl, are risking their lives because these drugs are almost 100 times as potent as heroin.

Based on the high usage and potential effects of opioids and opiates, it is understandable that employers target these drugs when employees are tested for illegal substances.

Marijuana, hash, and other cannabis

These drugs are very common. In fact, employees some consume them on a daily basis, and they believe it has little or no effect on their job performance. While this might be true in some instances, most workers are affected by marijuana, hash, and other cannabis. Their reaction times are much slower, and this results in them jeopardizing the safety of themselves and their coworkers.

In the United States, acceptance of cannabis is so high that it has been legalized in some cities and states. This legalization paves the way for employee usage in workplaces. Based on the potential for abuse, it is understandable that employers test workers for marijuana, hash, and other cannabis in their systems.

Liquor, beer, and other alcohol

Establishments all over the world sell alcohol. This makes it easy for people to get a drink, and it also makes it easy for them to abuse drinking. Unfortunately, that abuse sometimes comes while employees are working…and alcohol and work are a dangerous combination in the vast majority of situations.

A lack of stability and the loss of the ability to concentrate are common side effects of alcohol. Rampant alcohol abuse can even cause memory loss. Nobody wants to work with someone who is drunk because they know that there can be serious consequences. Bad experiences with drunken individuals cause people to turn in coworkers who are drinking on the job. In short, drinking at work is never a good thing, and that is why employers target alcohol when they drug test their employees.

Speed and other amphetamines

Amphetamines are used by employees because they provide energy to get through the workday. This might seem logical to some people, but, in reality, it makes no sense at all. Once a dependency develops, more and more of these drugs are needed to maintain the desired energy level…and the effort required to meet this need can be all-consuming. This effort takes precedence over everything else, including showing up for work and performing job tasks safely and productively. When the effects diminish, employees become lethargic and depressed; thereby resulting in them being unproductive when they are not high. Ultimately, this leads to wanting more amphetamines to reproduce the energetic feeling, and a vicious cycle begins.

Employers recognize that the use of amphetamines decreases productivity while increasing safety risks. For this reason, they target these drugs when testing their employees for substances in their bodies. This is understandable because it makes good business sense from a safety and economic standpoint.

Cocaine and other stimulants

Cocaine is a drug that was widely used in the 1980s. It was thought of as a stimulant that could keep people active for long hours without getting tired. They were able to socialize with others while remaining the "life of the party." However, few people realized the downside to this powerful drug. Eating and sleeping patterns were altered, causing people to become irritable, lose weight, and feel lethargic after the effects of the cocaine started to diminish. The crash was so severe some people experienced depression and suicidal thoughts.

Cocaine abuse is not as prevalent as it was a few decades ago, but it still exists…and it still destroys people's lives. Unfortunately, the use of cocaine and other stimulants occurs in workplaces all over the United States. Employees under the influence of this drug often make mistakes and miss work regularly.

After the issue involving cocaine abuse was recognized by the public, many leaders of organizations began implementing drug testing that targeted cocaine and other stimulants to root out the problem.

Now that you have an understanding of the drugs organizations test for, we can move on to a discussion on the methods used to detect these substances. The next section examines the various types of drug testing used by organizations to determine if employees have illegal substances in their systems.

Testing methods

Substances cannot be detected in employees' bodies without testing methods. These methods need to be accurate and authorized by a governing body if the results are to be used against employees in any way. For example, a manager cannot simply look at an employee and determine that they are high on PCP regardless of that employee's behavior. There needs to be scientific proof that PCP is in the employee's system, and that proof comes from approved testing methodology.

There are several different ways to test employees for illegal drug use. Approved methods include an analysis of:

Urine

This is probably the most well-known method of drug testing. Employees simply urinate in a container and their urine is then analyzed by a laboratory technician. This procedure might seem like there is a lot of room for mistakes, but there are rules in place that must be adhered to for every sample collected. A container designed to securely house the sample is used along with a tamper-resistant cap, and a "chain of custody" is followed to prevent potential laboratory errors. This procedure, while not foolproof, has proven effective and is used by organizations all over the world.

Unfortunately, urine testing can produce false positives. False positives erroneously make employees look as if they are ingesting illegal drugs, and this is embarrassing for the employee and the employer. Additionally, the amount of substance found is not determined nor is the length of time that it has been in the employee's body. Regardless of the negatives associated with urine testing, it does a good job confirming the presence of drugs and can be performed at a low cost to organizations.

Hair

This type of drug testing is not necessarily in the mainstream, but it is becoming an increasingly popular method of analysis used by organizations. The major reason for its popularity is the lengthy window of detection. It can detect drug use for up to 90 days, which is valuable for determining if employees are habitual users. It is also valuable for detecting stimulants such as cocaine due to the accurate results. Since cocaine is never consumed legally, the 90-day window does a good job of discovering this type of drug abuse. However, the negatives of this testing include the high cost and the lengthy amount of time required to complete the analysis.

Saliva

Saliva testing involves an analysis of an employee's saliva for residual drugs, and it is a good choice when there is a legitimate reason to believe that an employee is consuming illegal substances. It works best when the employees work onsite, such as those employed in manufacturing facilities and warehouses.

The pros of saliva testing are that it is fairly tamper-proof, making it difficult for employees to cheat, and it is fairly inexpensive. However, the cons of this type of testing are its inability to measure the frequency of use and the fact that it cannot detect drug use beyond 48 hours. Based on these pros and cons, the test is most valuable when an employee appears to be experiencing the effects of illegal substances.

Breath

This method tests for alcohol intoxication. While alcohol consumption is legal for a person who reaches a specified age, employees are not allowed to be drunk on the job.

Most people are familiar with breath testing being used by police officers on suspected drunk drivers, but it is also used by some employers to monitor the alcohol use of their workforces. However, depending on the work rules, employees might have a right to refuse to take a breath test, whereas motorists must submit to the testing or automatically lose their licenses.

The advantages of breath testing are accurate readings and fast results. However, problems can also occur. Belching, for example, can cause the results to be erroneously high, meaning employees could lose their jobs or be disciplined under false pretenses. Despite the potential problems involved with breath testing, it is a popular choice for measuring the alcohol level in people's bodies.

Blood

Blood testing provides is an accurate test for detecting substances in employees' bodies at the time their blood is drawn. They are a better indicator of recent drug consumption than urine, but there is a limited detecting window because most drugs move from the blood into the urine in a relatively short period of time. Add to this the need for specialized equipment, the invasiveness of the test, and the time required to obtain results, and it is understandable why most organizations use alternative methods for substance testing of their employees.

Sweat

This is likely the least common method of testing in workplaces. It typically involves placing a patch over a person's skin for a predetermined time period (usually no more than two weeks). It measures residual drugs in the sweat to determine if illegal substances were used while the patch was worn.

Sweat testing is an alternate choice for monitoring drugs used when urine testing is not practical, such as monitoring convicted criminals who are on parole. However, it has limited use for employees of companies because those employees can supply daily urine samples and employee rights activists protest wearing anything for lengthy time periods…especially if the designated employee has not been found guilty of a crime.

All of the above methods are capable of detecting drugs in employees' bodies. However, detection should not be the main concern of management because it does not address the root cause. Instead, prevention should be the ultimate goal because it attacks the root cause; thereby reducing the need for detection and saving organizations money, time, stress, and headaches. The importance of prevention makes it the focus of the next section.

Prevention

One positive aspect of drug abuse is that it can be prevented, and prevention is something leadership in every company should address. Prevention stops problems before they occur by treating the cause rather than the symptoms, and the time and money spent are justified by the time and money saved in the future. Unfortunately, it can be difficult to implement preventative measures, and that is why some companies choose to ignore the reality of their drug problems.

One measure of prevention involves communication. This measure might appear cliché or overused because communication is important for the prevention of all problems in organizations. If employees did not communicate, then tasks would not get accomplished and goals would not be achieved. However, despite these obvious facts, many organizations fail to communicate the importance of drug abuse. Employees are not aware of the powerful impact that drug abuse has on their productivity and safety. They need to know that it is no laughing matter, and coworkers who are stoned on the job negatively affect everyone who works with or around them.

Drug prevention communication with workforces can take place in a variety of ways. Witten, oral, and electronic communication channels are all effective in helping employees understand the importance of drug abuse. The following breaks down these channels for better understanding:

Written

Signage, letters, memos, and handouts are examples of using written channels of communication. Written communication is valuable because it puts documented information in front of employees for reading. This type of communication is advantageous over oral communication because "he said, she said" situations do not result in misunderstandings regarding what transpired are minimized.

Oral

Meetings and word-of-mouth discussions, both formal and informal, are examples of oral communication with employees. Oral communication sometimes works better than written communication because employees have the opportunity to ask questions regarding the subject matter. This question-asking clarifies various aspects of the drug abuse discussion; thereby making it easier to implement and maintain the prevention program.

Electronic

Email, instant messaging, texting, tweeting, and various forms of social media are all examples of this channel of communication. Electronic communication is valuable because information can be distributed to the masses in a matter of seconds, and employees can peruse the information when it is convenient rather than taking the time necessary to assemble for a meeting or read a memo. Additionally, electronic communication allows for the asking and answering of questions via forums and discussion boards. Last, but certainly not least, this type of communication channel allows for questions to be asked anonymously, and this is important for people who are intimidated by groups or large gatherings.

One important fact about electronic communication is that it is preferred by younger employees who grew up with it. They tend to think of oral and written communication channels as somewhat archaic and prefer the convenience of electronic discussion. In short, these employees appreciate the value of social media, so its value cannot be underestimated by organizational leaders.

All of the above channels of communication provide information that helps employees prevent drug abuse in their workplaces. Depending on the circumstances, one channel might be better than another…and sometimes a combination of these channels is the most effective way to communicate.

Another method of prevention is the use of pre-determined roles played by management and non-management members of organizations. The following are descriptions of these roles for better understanding:

Management

This includes upper management, lower management, and human resource management. Each of these is broken down below for a better understanding of specific roles.

Upper management – Drug prevention programs start at the top of organizations. Upper management personnel design and implement drug abuse programs that set the tone for the entire organization. They also incorporate strategies that support these programs and increase their chances of success. Their goal is to make the drug abuse programs simple and effective so all employees have an understanding of what is expected of them.

Lower management – These individuals are responsible for implementing and upholding the rules that are put in place by upper management. Their role is to understand the drug prevention program, communicate it to their employees while answering questions, and provide feedback to their bosses about its successes and failures. In reality, lower-level managers act as "drug abuse police" because they are charged with making sure employees adhere to the rules set in place.

Human resource managers – Human resource managers have an important role in terms of preventing drug abuse. They are responsible for the safety and well-being of employees, so they must work to stop drug abuse from occurring. They do this by implementing programs and providing information. For example, they implement employee assistance programs that show where employees and their families can get help with the mental and physical health problems associated with drug abuse. They also provide information about the symptoms of drug abuse, its effects on productivity, and how it can be prevented.

Non-management

This refers to employees other than those in management positions, which is typically most of the workforce. It also includes unions that are not members of the organizations they serve, but they play a part in drug abuse prevention. The roles of employees and unions are as follows:

Employees – This refers to the rank-and-file employees who perform the daily tasks necessary to help organizations reach goals and objectives. These individuals need to understand the importance of a drug-free workplace and discuss that importance with their coworkers. They also need to take responsibility for doing what is required of them and understand the resources available to them; thereby preventing roadblocks from hindering the success of the drug abuse program. The responsibilities of this role might seem simple and common sense based, but, in reality, they can be quite challenging for those who assume them.

Unions - Unions play a significant role in drug abuse prevention. These organizations are not completely made up of employees or managers, but they have a major influence on workforce policies and procedures. They typically have the trust of employees because they are looking out for those employees' best interests….something that management does not always appear to do. When unions support drug prevention programs, those programs are much more likely to be accepted by rank-and-file employees. Without union cooperation, drug prevention programs risk failure. Union officials understand the importance of drug prevention programs for the employees they represent, and that is why they are usually willing to help those programs succeed.

The last, and possibly most important, method of prevention involves commitment and support. There needs to be a shared sense of responsibility where all employees, regardless of their position on the organizational chart, do their part. However, these employees will not share that sense of responsibility if it does not start at the top of the organization. Upper management needs to be committed to preventing drug abuse and create a culture that moves in a drug-free direction. The "do as I say, not as I do" style of management does not work because contradictory actions trickle down the hierarchical ladder to the rank-and-file employees. Additionally, programs and strategies need to be assessed and changed if they are not working as designed. The entire commitment and support process can be challenging, but it is necessary for the success of drug prevention programs.

Summary

Drug abuse runs rampant in organizations all over the world, and it negatively impacts workplace productivity and safety. Without proper prevention programs in place, this problem could spiral into something that cannot be controlled...and everyone will pay the price.

This book focuses on drug abuse in organizations. It explains why management subjects employees to drug testing, analyzes the most common drugs targeted, explores the various testing methods available, and suggests methods of prevention. The text is informational and educational, and it is written for easy understanding at all reader levels.

Congratulations! You now understand more about drug abuse in organizations....a growing problem in workplaces all over the world.

www.ingramcontent.com/pod-product-compliance
Lightning Source LLC
Chambersburg PA
CBHW020435220526

45464CB00002B/711